I needed Dr. Caracciolo's book during Seminary did not prepare me for the issues related to the aging process. His wisdom would have prevented many of the mistakes I made in those early pastorates. I cannot be more emphatic, this book should be required reading for pastoral care classes in Bible colleges and seminaries. Denominational leaders should see that each of their pastors have a copy.

FRANK SCURRY, RETIRED PRESIDENT
CAROLINA GRADUATE SCHOOL OF DIVINITY

Rick Caracciolo fills a societal need with *The Challenges of Caregiving: Seeing, Serving, Solving*. This is an important resource for those who minister to or care for the elderly, especially young church pastors and their staff. His book offers solid information to help caregivers improve the quality of life of aging parents, congregants, and other caregivers working collectively to resolve life issues often brought on by natural aging. Dr. Caracciolo not only helps caregivers identify issues, he also shares how to lovingly honor and serve the elderly through the later years of life by solving care issues. This book will assist the professional and the layperson in improving the quality of life of aging adults and giving peace of mind to caregivers across the spectrum.

DR. EDDIE G. GRIGG, PRESIDENT
CHARLOTTE CHRISTIAN COLLEGE AND THEOLOGICAL SEMINARY

"Rick Caracciolo has provided a thorough treatment of crucial issues related to elderly caregiving. It is biblical, well-researched, and comes from several years of experience in the field. This will be a valuable resource in the years ahead as our population ages and families seek to serve their loved ones in their later years. While some families do not know where to even begin on these issues, or they get stuck at some point in the process, Dr. Caracciolo takes the reader from start to finish in the important ministry to the elderly. Families, counselors, and pastors will find this book beneficial."

DR. WESLEY C. MCCARTER
PROFESSOR, CHARLOTTE THEOLOGICAL SEMINARY
PASTOR, RURAL HALL CHRISTIAN CHURCH

This book is a must read! My husband and I are the primary care takers of my parents, and their minds and bodies are failing fast. I wish I had this book several years ago.

ELLEN PHILLIPS
CAREGIVER AND BABY BOOMER

"This book is a must read for anyone who has aging family members or who is aging themselves. It is a practical, supportive guide with a spiritual foundation to navigate the decisions that are faced when creating a plan for care giving. Thoughtful questions are posed and resources provided to assist in this journey."

DR. CYNTHIA DAVIES, ED.D
PRINCIPAL NEBO ELEMENTARY
PAULDING COUNTY SCHOOL DISTRICT

"Rick Caracciolo has written a must-read book dealing with the aging process and how to care for ourselves and others as we find it approaching."

DR. MARK CROOK,
DEAN OF PSYCHOLOGY AND CHRISTIAN COUNSELING
LOUISIANA BAPTIST UNIVERSITY

This book was enlightening, compassionate and educationally relevant especially to those of us in the middle stages of life that are beginning to care for our aging parents.

PAREN ARCHER,
PHYSICAL THERAPIST

THE CHALLENGES OF CAREGIVING: SEEING, SERVING, SOLVING

THE CHALLENGES OF CAREGIVING: SEEING, SERVING, SOLVING

Rick Caracciolo

ELM HILL

A Division of
HarperCollins Christian Publishing

www.elmhillbooks.com

The Challenges of Caregiving: Seeing, Serving, Solving

Published in Nashville, Tennessee, by Elm Hill, an imprint of Thomas Nelson. Elm Hill and Thomas Nelson are registered trademarks of HarperCollins Christian Publishing, Inc.

Elm Hill titles may be purchased in bulk for educational, business, fund-raising, or sales promotional use. For information, please e-mail SpecialMarkets@ ThomasNelson.com.

All Scripture quotations, unless otherwise indicated, are taken from the Holy Bible, New International Version˚, NIV˚. Copyright © 1973, 1978, 1984, 2011 by Biblica, Inc.˚ Used by permission of Zondervan. All rights reserved worldwide. www.Zondervan. com. The "NIV" and "New International Version" are trademarks registered in the United States Patent and Trademark Office by Biblica, Inc.˚

Scripture quotations marked KJV are from the King James Version. Public domain.

Scripture quotations marked THE MESSAGE are from *The Message*. Copyright © by Eugene H. Peterson 1993, 1994, 1995, 1996, 2000, 2001, 2002. Used by permission of NavPress. All rights reserved. Represented by Tyndale House Publishers, Inc.

Sample copies of Advance Directives and other materials taken from www.caringinfo. com are used with permission by National Hospice and Palliative Care Organization.

Library of Congress Cataloging-in-Publication Data

Library of Congress Control Number: 2019939772

ISBN 978-1-595559258 (Paperback)
ISBN 978-1-595559869 (Hardbound)
ISBN 978-1-595558763 (eBook)

DEDICATION

I would like to dedicate this book to God Almighty who is bringing me through this aging journey. Secondly, I am dedicating this work to my wife; Marguerite who has encouraged me along the way. She is a helpmate and a perpetual woman of God. She has been a true example of what a caregiver should be and is to those she is a caregiver for.
I would also like to thank Katie Nunn, Marvin Nunn, Phillip Toliver and Don Smith each who have been positive examples of what a caregiver should be in different life circumstances. Last but not least my granddaughter Za'Niyah who is the joy in our lives, puts a pep in our steps and brings love to our hearts. Thank you. God bless you.

CONTENTS

CHAPTER 1

AGING GRACEFULLY

"Then the LORD God formed a man from the dust of the ground and breathed into his nostrils the breath of life, and the man became a living being"

(GENESIS 2:7, NIV)

C omic book superheroes are capable of incredible acts, displaying superhuman feats, as we have seen on the silver screen and on the pages of comic books. Ordinary people, however, have also shown super-human strength and courage in extreme circumstances. For instance, Jim, who had been blind from birth, heard his eighty-four-year-old neighbor Annie Smith yelling for help. Jim was able to follow along the fence to her house, and when he reached the front door there was smoke and heat from a fire. Even under the most harrowing conditions he was still able to get into the house and pull her out of the front door. In another heroic deed, a daughter was able to rescue her father when he was crushed under his car while working underneath it. The jack suddenly slipped and fell on the man, crushing his chest. His daughter heard the noise when the jack slipped and trapped her father underneath. The twenty-two-year-old daughter was able to lift the car weighing several tons off her father. She then began providing first aid to him while waiting for emergency services.[1] Man is able to perform extraordinary acts during extraordinary times.

God has created man in His own image; we are fearfully and wonderfully made. God has made each and every one of us unique individuals and we are made in His image. We have different skin colors, hair colors, body shapes, and sizes, but we are all God's children. God knew who we were even before we were born, as Psalm 139:13 states, "For you created my inmost being; you knit me together in my mother's womb." The human body is so intriguing and intricate that only a loving God could have created man. Man is the only species whose life span is known to expand decades past its reproductive years. What makes man so special? The main substance of the human body is water, which accounts for 70–85 percent. At first glance the human body seems almost unimpressive, because it is made up of water and a few simple chemicals:

- Carbon: This is a chemical also found in diamonds and coal. A fifth of our body is coal.
- Iron: Iron makes the blood red. The human body has enough iron to make a small nail.
- Phosphorus: This can be found in our bones and teeth.
- Sodium and chlorine: These two chemicals make salt. The human body is ⅓ as salty as seawater.
- Potassium: This can be found in our bodily fluids. It is also used in some varieties of soap.
- Nitrogen: This chemical is important to our muscles and is also the main ingredient in the air.

If our bodies were recycled and the metals extracted from our remains, we would be worth about ten dollars. However, we are more than singly listed elements, chemicals, and liquid. There are over twenty commonplace elements that can be found in the earth's dust. In the body these elements

---

[1] "10 Superhuman Feats of Ordinary People," accessed December 26, 2017, http://www. learning-mind.com/superhuman-feats-of-ordinary-people/.

are combined in so many different ways that we are actually made up of thousands upon thousands of complex chemical compounds. Even more remarkable is the fact that the human body is not just a static jumble of chemicals, but a dynamic, highly organized, marvelously designed living organism. It constructs itself. It grows, acts and reacts, regulates its own activities, and keeps its parts in fairly good repair.[2]

- The cells and skin. In the human body there are 75–100 trillion cells divided into about 100 different categories. About 50,000 tiny flakes of dead skin drop off one's body every minute.[3] The average person has a total of six pounds of skin. The main job of the skin is to keep one's internal organs from drying up and to prevent harmful bacteria from getting inside the body.
- The nervous system. The human body has 93,200 miles of nerves throughout. The brain begins to lose thousands of neurons a day by age thirty.[4] These cells are not replaced when they die, and by the time we reach the age of eighty, our brains will weigh about 7 percent less than they did in our prime. What does all of this mean? Mental skills decline and tasks become more difficult, reaction time increases, our perception of heat and cold decreases, and we find it harder to keep our balance.[5]
- The cardiovascular system. The heart loses about 1 percent of its reserve pumping capacity each year after the age of thirty, reducing the amount of oxygen delivered throughout the body. The heart has four chambers and is about the size of a closed fist. It beats an average of 100–120 times a minute, 6,000 times in an hour, and 144,000 times a day.

---

2   Alma E. Guinness, ed., *ABC's of the Human Body* (USA: Reader's Digest, 1987), 22.

3   Caroline Bingham, *The Human Body* (New York, New York: DK Publishers, 2003), 10.

4   Penny Smith, ed., *First Human Body Encyclopedia* (New York, New York: DK Publishing, 2003), 33.

5   Unknown, "Why We Get Old," *Harvard Health Letter*, October 1992.

- The respiratory system. As our lungs age, they are no longer able to inflate or deflate completely because they have become less elastic. The left lung is smaller than the right lung to allow room for the heart. We take about 23,000 breaths each day.[6]

- The musculoskeletal system. There are 206 bones in the body and about 650 of our muscles are wrapped around the bones of the skeleton.[7] The muscles in the human body make up 40 percent of the body's weight. Muscles can contract to ⅓ of their size. It takes seventeen facial muscles to smile and forty muscles to frown. The muscles in our faces allow us to make 10,000 different facial expressions.[8] The skeletal system as a whole continues to maintain and replace itself, along with specific cells; osteoclast cart off old bone, and osteoblast replace it. The amount of new bone formed will depend on the body's demands for skeletal support. When an individual is confined to bed, weight bearing requirements decrease as a result of physical inactivity. Muscle mass and strength decline as we age due to a loss of muscle fibers and the nerves that stimulate them. Men and women tend to lose bone mass as they age. This process usually begins earlier and proceeds more rapidly in women, owing to a reduction in estrogen levels as menopause nears.[9]

- The digestive system. Tooth enamel is the hardest and toughest substance in the body. Teeth contain no living cells, so they cannot repair themselves if damaged. The digestive system holds up better than most of the body's other systems. Like the muscular structures, the alimentary organs (esophagus, stomach, small intestine, and colon) lose tone with age. The regular contractions that propel food through them become

---

[6]   Bingham, *The Human Body*, 22.

[7]   Smith, *First Human Body Encyclopedia*, 24.

[8]   Bingham, *The Human Body*, 17.

[9]   Unknown, "Why We Get Old."

less frequent and less efficient. The other digestive organs also begin to slow with age. The gallbladder becomes sluggish in releasing bile into the small intestine, increasing the probability of gallstones. The liver shrinks with age and receives a smaller blood supply than previously, and needs more time to metabolize drugs and alcohol.

- The immune system. The immune system becomes hampered by the gradual degeneration of the thymus. The thymus is a small gland in the neck responsible for helping coordinate the body's defense system. This gland reaches its maximum size by puberty and then begins to shrink shortly after, virtually disappearing by the time an individual reaches old age. This loss, in turn, leaves the immune system less resilient and less capable of fighting off diseases and infections.

- The excretory system. The kidneys begin to have a gradual reduction of blood flow, along with a decrease in the nephrons (filtering units), which impairs its ability to extract waste from the blood and concentrate them into urine as we get older. The kidneys will then require more water to excrete the same amount of waste that they did when the body was younger. In addition bladder capacity declines as we get older, which in turn necessitates more frequent urination.

- The sensory system. The five senses also begin to diminish with age. The lenses of the eyes are not as elastic and are not able to change, focus, or redirect on objects as quickly, and in some instances not at all. The sense of taste decreases as the number of taste buds decrease. There are four different types of taste: bitter, sour, salty, and sweet. We become less able to appreciate a wide range of flavors and taste as we grow older. Our sense of taste becomes less discriminating and our ability to distinguish different foods from one another diminishes. The sense of smell declines as one becomes more increasingly oblivious to delicate fragrances. The sense of hearing varies with each individual, just as our vision does. The three bones in the ear are the smallest in the human body. The stapes is the smallest and is no larger than a grain of rice.

- The endocrine system. The hormone-secreting glands shrink as we get older, but it seems their performance is not affected. Age alone does not change the output of the thyroid hormone that regulates metabolism, the output of adrenalin, which coordinates the body's response to stress, or that of pituitary hormones, which stimulate the thyroid, adrenal glands, and ovaries. The aging pancreas secretes insulin to regulate glucose, so that the metabolism can respond to sudden increases in blood sugar as readily as when younger, even though an increased level of glucose is required to jolt it into action.

If all of our systems declined at the same time, the outlook would be pretty bleak. Each system ages according to its own timetable, and this can vary quite dramatically from person to person. Some of the factors that affect the timetable are genes, lifestyle, and personal well-being. The human body is truly fearfully and wonderfully made.

Here They Come Ready or Not, the Baby Boomers

In the late spring they seem to be more prevalent. They can be found almost anywhere you go, especially in the mid to late afternoon. It appears that you see more of them at the beginning of the week. Many times you will spot them in small groups of two to three, and occasionally in a pack of five to six. They can be found in the grocery stores, the malls, parks, and even in churches. You can distinguish them from others by their grayish-color heads, and they travel at varying speeds. Their numbers are astonishing; they are living longer and expected to grow to over 75 million. Each week more than 200 of them reach the age of 100.[10]

Baby boomers, that's who! They were born over a span of nineteen years, beginning in 1946 until 1964, creating quite a diverse breed. Some were born in the quiet 50s, others the turbulent 60s, and still others in the economically stressed 70s. In the year 2011, the first wave of baby boomers began turning sixty-five years of age.[11] Many baby boomers are finding out that they are not living in the "Age of Aquarius" anymore, but in the "sandwich" phase of their lives. Boomers will now find themselves adjusting to the new rhythms of the boomer life cycle. A significant number of boomers will have to juggle multiple demands, from raising children or grandchildren, working full time, and also assisting an aging parent(s). Their plates are full and they will need an outlet. As the baby boomers age they will invite society to reevaluate what it means to be old, including one's personal expectations, as well as those of families', churches', communities', and institutions'. The questions will be related to the well-being of older adults. In order to understand who we are discussing, it would be good to know how each generation is defined and what their ages are.

1. "Seniors" were born in 1926 and earlier.
2. "Builders" were born in 1927 to 1945.
3. "Baby boomers" were born in 1946 to 1964.
4. "Busters" were born in 1965 to 1983.

Are these people the responsibility of the government, family, community, Church? Or are they responsible for themselves?

---

[10] Federal Interagency Forum on Aging-Related Statistics, August 2016, accessed December 14, 2017, https://agingstats.gov/docs/LatestReport/Older-Americans-2016-Key-Indicators-of-WellBeing.pdf.

[11] Ibid.

Aging Is Natural—Not Our Enemy

Man's perception of aging and how aging is accepted has not changed dramatically since the beginning of time. Over the last 230 years, man's life expectancy has increased to what the psalmist spoke of in Psalm 90:10, "Our days may come to seventy years, or eighty, if our strength endures; yet the best of them are but trouble and sorrow, for they quickly pass, and we fly away." Our life expectancy now is about seventy-eight years old. By the time we reach this age we have started slowing down, not as strong or as stable as we were in the past. Everyone has started slowing down, and they are not as quick and mobile as they were when they were younger.

Bathauer wrote, "Psychologists tell us that all of life is made up of continuous changes from childhood all the way to old age."[12] The last twenty years of life, the stage we call old age, brings about almost as many changes as the first twenty years. Changes in the latter part of life are usually more than all the changes during the first twenty years of life, because they carry the threat of loss, disability, or other degenerative conditions.[13]

Although Christian counselors are generally trained in the spiritual and mental aspects of health, as the graying of America continues at an accelerated rate, the Christian counselor is going to need the tools and resources to counsel in this area. Aging will be an area that will affect everyone. The caregiver can benefit personally by having an understanding of physical disabilities and the human body. Also by having the knowledge of where to retrieve additional updated information for a client is a blessing to all. During this very stressful period in which there is limited time to make major decisions, it helps reassure the counselee that there is someone who cares and is trying to help. Also by gaining these skills and knowledge, it will allow the counselor to truly counsel the whole person. He is now able to help in a spiritual, mental, and physical

---

[12] Ruth M. Bathauer, *Parent Care: Fear and Losses of the Elderly* (Ventura, CA: Regal Books, 1984), 99.

[13] L. Gelhaus, "Boomers Prefer Aging at Home," *Provider Magazine* 30 (2004).

dimension. Again, it is not expected that every counselor will become a specialist in aging or a gerontologist. The expectation is that they will minimally become a resource for those in need, or be able to refer clients to a Christian counselor who specializes in the area of aging issues and concerns.

Man has always had an improper view of immortality from the beginning of time. He has not wanted to face the fact that he cannot do the activities he could in his earlier years as he gets older and closer to his end days. Thousands and thousands of years ago Solomon wrote in Ecclesiastes 12:1–7 (*The Message*):

> Honor and enjoy your Creator while you're still young, before the years take their toll and your vigor wanes, before your vision dims and the world blurs and the winter years keep you close to the fire. In old age, your body no longer serves you so well. Muscles slacken, grip weakens, joints stiffen. The shades are pulled down on the world. You can't come and go at will. Things grind to a halt. The hum of the household fades away. You are wakened now by bird-song. Hikes to the mountains are a thing of the past. Even a stroll down the road has its terrors. Your hair turns apple-blossom white, adorning a fragile and impotent matchstick body. Yes, you're well on your way to eternal rest, while your friends make plans for your funeral. Life, lovely while it lasts, is soon over. Life as we know it, precious and beautiful, ends. The body is put back in the same ground it came from. The spirit returns to God, who first breathed it.

The question now is, what does old age mean? The definition and perception of old and aging have changed and been redefined over the last 150 years. The aging process has contributed to this confusion about the appropriate performance or expected roles and activities of older adults. This in part has evolved because the United States was primarily an agricultural society, then mostly an industrial society, and now primarily a technological society that has changed the experience of aging.[14] A recent development is retirement. In years gone by, people rarely lived long enough to retire, and those who did often had ongoing responsibilities. We need to have a proper spiritual, historical, and cultural context for understanding the process and why it is important. As Achenbaum and Stern have stated, "We cannot discuss old age without some sense of trend, of where we are coming from and where we are heading."[15] Now as life expectancy has increased significantly, man has even less of a tendency to accept the fact that he and his family should research and investigate potential options for emergency situations in their later years of life. If and when these services are needed, the individual and family members will feel more comfortable under pressure in making a decision if they are prepared.

We Are Getting Older as a Country

Life expectancy is a summary of the overall health of a population. It represents the average number of years of life remaining to a person at a given age if death rates were to remain constant. In the United States improvements in health have resulted in increased life expectancy and contributed to the growth of the older population over the past century. Americans are living longer than centuries before. The growth of the population sixty-five years of age and over affects many aspects of our society, challenging policy makers, families, businesses, and health-care providers, among others, to meet the needs of aging individuals. During the twentieth century the older population grew from three million to 46 million in 2014, accounting for just over 15 percent of the population. The oldest population, those eighty-five years and over, grew from just over 100,000 in 1900 to six million in 2014.

The baby boomers, those born between 1946 and 1964, started turning sixty-five in 2011. The number of older individuals will increase dramatically during the period between the year 2014 and the year 2030. The older

---

[14] Betty R. Bonder and Marilyn B. Wagner, *Functional Performance in Older Adults* (Philadelphia, PA: F. A. Davis, 1994), 5.

[15] Ibid.

population in 2030 is expected to be twice as large as their counterparts in 2000, growing from 35 million to 74 million and representing nearly 21 percent of the total U.S. population. The growth rate of the older population is projected to slow after 2030, when the last of the baby boomers enter its ranks. From the year 2030 and beyond, the proportion age sixty-five years and over will be relatively stable at around 21 percent, even though the absolute number of people age sixty-five years and is projected to continue to grow. In addition the oldest segment of the elderly population is projected to grow rapidly after 2030, when the baby boomers move into this age group.[16]

The United States Census Bureau projects that the population aged eighty-five years and over could grow from 4.2 million in 2000 to nearly 21 million by 2050. Some researchers predict that death rates among the elderly could decline more rapidly than is reflected in the United States Census Bureau's projections, which could lead to a faster growth of this age group. The proportion of the population age sixty-five years and over varies by state. The population is partly affected by the state fertility and mortality rates and by the number of older and younger people who migrate to and from the state. The highest proportion of people age sixty-five years and over in the year 2002 was Florida, with 17 percent. Pennsylvania and West Virginia also had high proportions of over 15 percent.

The proportion of the population age sixty-five years and over varies even more by county. In 2014, 53 percent of Sumter County, Florida's, population was sixty-five years and over. In other areas of Florida there were several counties where the proportion was over 30 percent. On the other end of the spectrum, in one Georgia county, the population sixty-five years and over was only 4.2 percent of the population.

In most countries of the world women outnumber men, and the United States is no exception. The proportion that is female increases with age. In 2014, women accounted for 56 percent of the population age sixty-five years and over and for 66 percent of the population age eighty-five years and over. The United States is fairly young for a developed country, with just 15 percent of its population age sixty-five years

---

[16] Federal Interagency Forum on Aging-Related Statistics.

and over. The older population made up more than 15 percent of the population in most European countries and just over 20 percent in Germany, Italy, and Greece.[17] Concerns about aging will be present in the United States and globally as the citizens of these countries get older.

Functioning in later years may be diminished due to illnesses, chronic diseases, mental abilities, or injuries limiting physical abilities. Older women, 31 percent, reported more problems than men, 18 percent, being unable to perform at least one of five activities. Physical-functioning problems were more frequent at older ages. Physical functioning was related to race, but not significantly.[18]

There are many factors, both internally and externally, that affect the choices that we make. Some of the internal factors that need to be considered are individual preferences, caregiver responsibilities, culture, family dynamics, and the individual's health condition. When weighing all of the factors in making a decision, an individual should consider both internal and external factors. Each individual and family member will have to determine and classify what they consider to be their priority for each factor or preference, whether internal or external, in relation to personal desires, requirements, and future needs.

The human life expectancy has been increasing significantly from thirty-seven years old in 1776, forty-seven years old in 1900, to seventy-nine years old in 2000. This is only the average life expectancy. A woman who lives to sixty-five years of age generally has another eighteen years' life expectancy, and a female who lives to be eighty-five years old averages another six years of life expectancy. However, aging like the future, has no predictable pattern. Some aging experts and gerontologists believe that the human life span will not go much beyond eighty-five years of age if there are no significant breakthroughs in the aging process. How realistic is it to believe that the aging process will stop? We have no way of determining when life expectancy and the aging process will come to a standstill. Time and time again man has thought he has broken the

---

[17] Ibid.

[18] Ibid.

code to aging, but to his dismay he has failed. "No one understands why we age, and there has been more than three hundred theories proposed that have a connection to aging."[19]

Old age is a mental attitude as well as a physical concern. Most people cringe when you discuss old age and getting older. Through the ages people have tried numerous ways to postpone old age. They have tried various foods, products, drinks, and support groups. They have tried traveling, to feel young and fulfilled. They apply creams, drink concoctions, follow charts, and enroll in so-called health programs to try to postpone old age. The older one becomes as a believer, the better one's life should be as a believer. God has a plan for us, and it is bigger than any problem life can produce. God's plan is that old age is the crowning glory of a person's lifetime. The Word of God shows that old age can have promise, productivity, vitality, confidence, and a great deal of happiness, providing that spiritual preparation has taken place during the younger years. Many individuals become old before their time because they have spent their whole life worrying about being prepared for old age. They have spent a significant amount of time during their life concentrating on how to prevent problems, many of which they have no control over when they get older.

A Spiritual Perspective on Aging

Some Bible scholars believe that the Bible indicates that there are three broad divisions of a lifetime. The period of youth lasts up to the age of forty years old. When Moses was around forty he began to sense his responsibility to Israel and to the Lord (Acts 7:23). Moses spent forty more years in training before he became the leader to the people of Israel. Moses did his great works during the years from eighty to 120. Paul wrote in 1 Timothy 4:12 (KJV): "Let no man despise thy youth." Timothy was in his thirties at this time. A man was healed, yet the Sanhedrin wanted to ridicule his testimony. In Acts 4:22, we find "the man was above 40 years

---

[19] Susan Shelly, *When It's Your Turn: Grown Children Caring for Aging Parents* (United States of America: Barnes & Noble, 2003), 103.

on whom this healing was shown," indicating he was mature enough to know what had happened.

The time from age forty to sixty is considered the middle-age period. Many believers accomplish a significant amount in the middle years. A sixty-year-old widow's retirement was turned into a full-time ministry of prayer supported by the Church (1 Timothy 5:9). The high-priest work-load was at its heaviest between thirty and fifty years of age.

The period of old age was from sixty years onward. At the age of ninety, Daniel was told to stop acting like a dead man and get going. A woman of eighty-four years in Luke 2:36–38 was very active in serving the Lord, and Abraham lived to 175, Isaac to 180, Sara to 127, and Ishmael to 137 years of age. In the past, old age was welcome and honored. Individuals were not thought of as having outlived their usefulness. As we age, get slower, and weaker, we should not give up. We should be active within our physical limits. It is time to use our wisdom and sage to advance those younger and celebrate our years that God has granted us. "Old age was not a defeat but a victory, not a punishment but a privilege."[20]

Even so, some of the unhappiest and most miserable old people can be Christians. They are grumpy, demanding, and obnoxious. They no longer have their youth to protect them. They are now out in the open for all to see. Proverbs 23:7 (KJV) so wisely says, "As a man thinks in his heart so is he." All of their lives, youth has been the excuse for their bad behavior, and now they do not have youth to hide behind. Exposed by old age, all their faults, habits, and characteristics are open for all to see. King Solomon wrote Ecclesiastes when he reached "old age." He had some advice to which the young could adhere to prevent heartache in their old age: "Find happiness when you are young" (Ecclesiastes 12:1). Then you can carry inner happiness from the Word of God that which does not depend upon conditions or circumstances within or around you, thus creating a fulfilling old age.

In Victor Frankel's book *Man's Search for Meaning*, he concluded that those who survive are those who make meaning from their situations

---

[20]   James M. Houston and Michael Parker, *A Vision for the Aging Church* (Downers Grove, Il: IVP Academic, 2011), 55.

and who find activities that give purpose even in the most hopeless circumstances.[21] He emphasized the necessity of finding meaning in life no matter what life involves. While an activity might be similar from one man to another, the meaning of the activity will differ based on the individual's characteristics, background, circumstances, and religious beliefs.

It Is Just Around the Corner

As we travel down the path of aging and caregiving, we are going to discover that making decisions and accepting the facts are not going to be as cut and dry as we would like. We are all made of the same chemicals and minerals, but we are each an individual who is made in the image of God. You will see as you read through this book that there will be some areas that have just the information you have been looking for, and another portion might not have anything you need now. The tendency is to skip over information we do not currently need and proceed on to what we are interested in and need at the minute. The advice is not to do that because what you do not need today you may need tomorrow. Remember, we all age at different rates and require information at various times because we are not the same as our spouses, families, and friends. Each person, each family member, each neighbor will have their own unique combination of needs. Everyone has different likes and dislikes, wants, needs, joys, and hurts. We are a people of adjectives, and when we must decide we have to pull all of our options together to weigh them out. We will review all the negative and positive areas that are affecting our loved ones and ourselves before we make a decision. The more information that you gather from this book, the easier it will be to choose which options are the best for your situations. The information in this book is like a smorgasbord. As you read through the book you will take and apply the information that you need now and put the other information on the back burner for a later date. The more you learn now, the more comfortable you will be when you make a decision because you will know that you have done all that you can at the time. You might not need to know about diverse types of housing options or caregiver burnout now, but it will be comforting to know something about it and where you can go to review the information.

---

[21] Victor E. Frankel, *Man's Search for Meaning* (Boston, MA: Beacon Press, 1962), 157.

We must tailor make decisions as a caregiver for the care receiver to produce the best end results for our loved ones. As you move forward remember to think about or even role play situations; see how the information can apply to your current or future situation. The statistics and facts in the book are not there to scare you. This information is there as a reminder that America is graying. You might not see it where you live right now, nor have family who requires assistance yet. We tend to think because something is not currently affecting us or we do not see it, maybe the information is just hyped up or overblown. As you read this book you will discover that is not the case. We are all going to be affected in some way as the baby boomers age past sixty-five years old. It is better to be prepared and know what to do than sitting on your hands and then be in panic mode because your aging family crept up on you all at once and need help now.

Purposeful Thought and Talk through Questions

Here is an opportunity to go deeper into the chapter. By using these questions, you have an opportunity to discuss scenarios and to think about different options through self-talk, counseling, or a small group session. These questions are not designed to be controversial or divisive. There are no right or wrong answers, because each individual and family have different life situations and experiences.

1. Do you believe the human body is "fearfully and wonderfully made"? Why, or why not?
2. What is your view on life expectancy?
3. Why might some individuals be unhappy during their later years? Can anything be done to help alleviate their unhappiness? If so, what?
4. What changes have you noticed in completing daily activities compared to when you were younger?
5. Do you think your family, church, and community are prepared for the aging baby boomers turning sixty-five years old? Why, or why not? Might you be affected?

CHAPTER 2

FAMILY MATTERS

"Remember the days of old, Consider the years of many generations. Ask your father, and he will show you; Your elders, and they will tell you"

(DEUTERONOMY 32:7)

It was beginning to be another one of those days. Joseph had to make a decision by the end of the day, and he still was not sure what to do. His parents were both second generation Irish Americans. His father had made him promise before he passed away that he would not put his mother in a nursing home. He was told since he was the oldest child, it was his family duty and responsibility to never to put his mother in a nursing home, just as his parents and grandparents before them had never let anyone put their parents in a nursing home for any reason.

His sister and mother never got along, so mom staying with her was out of the question. His little brother Mike lived in another state, so he seemed to be out of the picture as far as taking in their mother. They had already told Joseph to do what he thought was best and that they would support his decision. It was not that he did not want to take care of his mother; it was he could not. He had been taking care of her and checking on her several times a week until this last episode. Her Alzheimer's disease was getting worse, and he was to the point he did not feel comfortable leaving her at home alone. Even with the home health aide who stayed with her for a few hours daily, things just were not right. This time mom got up and wandered outside to take a walk and visit some of her old neighbors at two thirty in the morning. Needless to say, the neighbors were none too happy, but they were understanding. What made the situation even worse was that the neighbors who mother had decided she wanted to visit had moved away years ago, and she did not remember.

Along with leaving a pan on the burning stove, she had also climbed on a chair and fallen off, breaking her arm. He never did know why she was climbing on the chair. Every time he had asked her why she was standing on the chair, he had not gotten a clear answer. "You know how I fell and broke my arm; I already told you. You are just trying to see if I remember," his mother would say. Joseph had taken the step stool out of the kitchen months ago, hoping to prevent something like this from happening. He never dreamed his mom would drag a chair into the kitchen and start climbing around, reaching into cabinets.

Each of those situations could have been worse, but since Joseph started visiting his mom twice a day he was able to divert each situation from being worse than it was. Besides visiting his mom, he also tried to call her between each visit to see how she was doing. He had been calling her daily for years, so that was nothing new. The pressure of the extra visits, telephone calls, and worrying about his mom was affecting his work and marriage. He had to decide, because the doctor had stated his mother was not able to safely live at home alone any longer. He had asked the physician when she had broken her arm the week before to give him a week to decide what to do.

Should he move his mother into his house with his wife and kids? Should he move her to an apartment so when she got better she could move back to her house? What about a nursing home with twenty-four-hour care? Is it possible that the Alzheimer's disease is likely to reverse? He knew he would have to make some hard decisions one day; he never dreamed it would be something like this. Why had his father asked him to promise he would not put his mother in a nursing home? Did he understand what he was asking him? Joseph certainly did not understand the impact or pressure he would feel years later when he nonchalantly answered his father with, "Yes, I will never put mom in a nursing home."

Same Facts, Different Decision

It can be difficult enough to make what we might call everyday decisions such as where to attend college, which mortgage company to use when purchasing a home, in which bank to open a checking and savings account, or whether or not it is time to change employers. All of these decisions can weigh heavily on us because they can have a significant impact on our lives for years to come. Does the college one wants to attend have the program that is best for them? What about the mortgage company one has decided to use to purchase their home? Did one understand their fine print? Is that the best interest rate and plan available or did one just take the first offer that came in the mail? Changing banks and opening a new checking and savings account can be very stressful. For every positive story one hears about a bank, there is a horror story someone else reports, such as a missing deposit, overdraft fees, or poor customer service. This leaves a person with no idea how to make the right choice.

If these everyday decisions can be that difficult when one is deciding what to do, then how does someone determine the best choices to make for a loved one? It is a heavy burden to make life-changing decisions for another person, all the while trying to be fair, unselfish, and have their best interest in mind. It is not a natural position to be in or to be put into. There are so many different factors to weigh when we are making decisions for a parent or loved one. This is not an especially easy position to be in. Our culture often shapes or influences our beliefs. The cultural beliefs that we may have been raised with may not be the norm today as they were forty years ago. When Joseph's father was younger, he may have heard horror stories about nursing homes from his parents who might have also made him promise not to put them in one. This could very well be why his father pressured him to make that promise. He may have never visited a nursing home, or never have heard another negative story about one. The father was passing along his culture, what he was taught and believed to be right at that time.

As we know, we might have to make the same decision as a person such as buying a car. We each have the same amount of money to purchase the vehicle but choose completely different vehicles. One person wants an SUV while the other a four-door; one chooses red and the other black; one chooses a sunroof, but the other does not. We each have preferences and different life events and history that play a part in our choices. On the outside, another person's decisions seem simple to make. In reality on the inside, it is tormenting, and there sometimes appears to be no right or straightforward answer. What we are left with is what we like to call "the lesser of two evils." This means we have a choice to make, and we do not like either of the options, but they are the only selections available. Today many of our beliefs and decisions are still influenced by our culture—right or wrong.[22]

Jesus Cares for His Mother from the Cross

"As Jesus was hanging on the cross, he spoke to his beloved friend and disciple, saying, 'Here is your mother.' From that time on, this disciple took her into his home."[23] Jesus entrusted the care of his mother Mary to John. Why was John and not one of his half-brothers asked to care for their mother? We know that Jesus was the eldest son and that being the eldest male child meant the responsibility of caring for His mother was His responsibility. Jesus was as concerned about His mother's spiritual welfare as her economic welfare. John was His beloved friend and believer, who was present at the crucifixion. It was an honor and great

---

[22] Beulla Wood, "A Theology of the Generations: Do People Still Risk Feudalism in the Family?" 23, no. 3 (Summer 2008), p. 27.

[23] *The New International Version* (Grand Rapids, MI: Zondervan, 2011), John 19:27.

responsibility spiritually and financially when John was asked to care for Mary, Jesus' mother, and bring her into his own house. During this time John 7:5 reminds us that none of Jesus' siblings believed in Him until after the resurrection. From the cross, Jesus spoke to His mother to ease the pain, and to let her know that everything was going to be all right. His words were heard and recorded for all mankind to hear. While He was on the cross dying for our sins, He was also providing for His mother and her earthly future. Jesus' concern is a vivid example that taking care of a parent or loved one is a tremendous responsibility.[24] When making a decision, we should try to be as informed as possible and make our decision based on the facts and knowledge that we have at that time. We can always second-guess ourselves and read about new techniques or procedures. In hindsight we did not have this information at the time of our decision. So as we move forward remember that we can only make decisions based on the information we have at the time.

Caregiving Facts to Think About

Caring for a parent can be very taxing and trying for the caregiver and their family. In many instances, the family member who is the primary caregiver is also the legal guardian, or party responsible for the parent. For our discussion, we will follow this same path. Many older Americans have their caregiving needs met by a family member. Almost three-quarters of the disabled elderly receiving caregiver services depend entirely upon family or other unpaid help. An estimated 18 million family caregivers spend an average of ten to fifteen hours a week assisting the elderly relative. About three-quarters of the caregivers are women, and most of them work outside the home. Many of them are raising children, and some have grandchildren. They are wedged between the responsibilities of caring for both younger and older generations; they are over extended, stressed, guilt-plagued, and financially squeezed. They are a

---

[24] Matthew Henry, "The Care He Took of His Mother," accessed November 1, 2017, https://www.wordsearchbible.com.

growing group that has been dubbed "the sandwich generation." They are the substances that are holding the older generation and the younger generation.[25] Caregiving can be divided into many tasks such as bathing, dressing, preparing a meal, or running errands. Caregiving is indeed a family activity. Family caregivers can be anyone from a spouse, child, grandchild, or other relatives. Family caregivers usually range in age from teenagers to senior adults.[26]

The Importance of Family Involvement

Before deciding to become the primary caregiver, one should set up a family meeting time, so concerns can be discussed and talked over with the immediate family household, and then the siblings and other family members if they are involved in the care of the individual. During the meeting, one should be sure to establish realistic goals and communicate with one's siblings and other family members regarding how many hours of help they will need to provide or how much they need to contribute each month financially. When an individual is aware of the commitment requested of them from the beginning, it is easier to get a truthful answer from them.

In addition the goals and expectations of the siblings and other family members will need to be considered when deciding to become the primary caregiver. The individual who is to become the primary caregiver should be sure that everyone who is onboard has made a commitment as to how they are going to help, and that he or she has heard them make that commitment firsthand. One cannot assume that a sibling or grandchild is going to help without hearing their verbal commitment. Even after an individual has said they will assist in caregiving duties, it is no

---

[25] Virginia Schomp, *Aging Parent Handbook: The Baby Boomer Dilemma* (New York, NY: Harper Collins Publishers, 1997), xv.

[26] Federal Interagency Forum on Aging-Related Statistics, "Older Americans 2016 Key Indicators of Well-Being," August 2016, accessed December 14, 2017, http://agingstats. gov/docs/LatestReport/Older-Americans-2016-Key-Indicators-of-WellBeing.pdf.

assurance that they will contribute help for any length of time. The financial, emotional, and physical demands of caregiving can be high, and the resulting stress or burden can threaten the ability of caregivers to maintain their efforts.[27] A person knows his family members and whether or not they are people who volunteer to help but never show up to do the job. One should not be fooled into thinking that people will change their characteristics when one is considering assisting with caregiving duties or being the primary caregiver.

Furthermore, as the primary caregiver, one should try to answer the concerns of all the individuals who will be assisting with caregiving duties. By answering their questions, they will feel more comfortable in knowing what is expected of them and they can keep the primary caregiver informed as to whether or not they can still follow through on their commitment. By answering the concerns of the other family volunteers who will be caregivers, one is better able to see if his caregiving plan is feasible and balances the many needs of family and work.

Caregiving Is Challenging and Important Work

Being a caregiver for a family member enrolls you in an informal group of individuals that has become one of the largest in the United States.[28] This group has similar life experiences, feelings, and attitudes. It is often the case that caregivers feel alone, unappreciated, abandoned, and guilty about the situation in which they are involved. Some caregivers have chosen to help out, and others were selected "de facto," meaning there was no one else available or willing to become the caregiver. Nearly one-third of these individuals became a caregiver in this manner. Many adult children took on the role of caregiver in this manner because there

---

[27] Federal Interagency Forum on Aging-Related Statistics, "Older Americans 2016 Key Indicators of Well-Being," August 2016, accessed December 14, 2017, http://agingstats.gov/docs/LatestReport/Older-Americans-2016-Key-Indicators-of-WellBeing.pdf.

[28] Susan Beerman and Judith Rappaport, *Eldercare 911: The Caregiver's Complete Handbook for Making Decisions* (Amherst, NY: Prometheus Books, 2002), 20.

was no one else available or willing to take on the task. The caregiver took on the role because they felt there were no other suitable alternatives at this time, such as a nursing home.[29]

Each caregiving situation is different, but each individual goes through some of the same emotional roller coaster of feelings. So what is normal in caregiving? "There is no normal… The key to coping and understanding your parent's changing needs is to learn to recognize actions and identify symptoms that fall outside of expected and acceptable changes."[30] As we age, we change, and it is often difficult for us to know when we are appreciated or might need to accept an offer of assistance. It is difficult for a person to ask for assistance doing a task that they have independently done for decades. Even though the caregiver means well, it can feel very dehumanizing to the care receiver to need help getting in and out of a chair, carrying groceries into the house, or remembering his or her street address. The care receiver, the parent, now needs help doing things they taught the child how to do. It is difficult to change caregiving roles and now become the one who is making decisions for our parent. In many instances we let others define us. "In society, our role is often viewed through the emotions we experience as a parent, sibling, brother, sister, children, friend and trusted adviser."[31] The loss of identity can cause someone to feel lost and lonely. Caregiving is not for the weak. Family caregivers know the individual they are considering taking upon the duties of caring for and have to be honest with themselves about the care receiver, siblings, spouse, and family if it is practical. The best option at the time might be to explore other housing because they might be more suitable at this time. In six months to a year, an evaluation of the current housing arrangement could be made, and one can decide if it is feasible to explore other options.

---

[29] Deborah M. Merrill, *Caring for Elderly Parents* (Westport, CT: Auburn House, 1997).

[30] Susan Beerman and Judith Rappaport. *Eldercare 911: The Caregiver's Complete Handbook for Making Decisions*, 46.

[31] Ibid., 39.

Family Dynamics

Family dynamics are unique to each family. On the outside situations from two families, even those related, are as different as night and day. When discussing family dynamics, it is best when making decisions one uses the facts and information known to be true, not what one hopes will happen. No two families are alike; each family can have multiple siblings and extended family groups. Each family has its groups, each of which has its own set of influences, personalities, and family dynamics. To get to the heart of the matter, it will take a focused and strong individual to sift through all of the chaff to get to the grain. When we start getting to the grain, that is where the real concerns and issues lay.

It can take a while to sift through the selfish concerns, anger, lack of forgiveness, and carnal man to reach the real issues at hand. The goal and end results should always be the same: to do what is best for the individual needing care. This is why it is so essential that when caregiving is being discussed, the focus has to stay on what is best for the care receiver. What is best does not necessarily entail the care receiver moving into the home of one of the children. Counseling individuals and family members concerning what the available housing options are and discussing different scenarios with them can be complicated. Ultimately the decision is theirs, and as counselors and pastors, we are conveyors of information, prayer, support, and peace. When assisting a family where we know the caregiver, care receiver, and family, it can be more difficult than counseling a family that we have just recently met. When a counselor or pastor is familiar with the family, one should be cautious about prejudicially presenting what they believe to be a very good idea or thinking, that one knows what is the best solution because they know the family members. One may know the family but still not know the family as well as they may think.

Having too strong of an opinion and pushing the family into something they may not want can be disastrous for the pastor-client relationship down the road. Unless the pastor or counselor knows that specific harm is being directed toward the care receiver, the decision rests with the family. It is at this point that one should be praying for the family if they have not already been doing so. The decision that was made can be from past issues they have not been able to resolve or an issue that we may know nothing about. Until the family's personal and spiritual conflicts are resolved, until we leave them at the foot of the cross, we will not be able to receive the truth.[32]

Furthermore, the family might be wavering and stalling when a situation calls for an immediate answer. An individual or family might be choosing options that are contrary to all advice and against the best interests of those concerned. It is not always easy to understand why people do what they do, or why they feel the way they do. Establishing causation may be one of the most challenging tasks facing a counselor. Some decisions, or lack thereof, are made because of retaliation, anger, or guilt, and others are due to personality temperament. Therefore causation is not always easy for the counselor to discern, but with prayer and the guidance of the Holy Spirit, they can know the truth. What is best may not always be what the individual or the family wants, however. When a caregiver is called upon or forced to make decisions for a parent who has always been domineering and challenging, it is not easy for this caregiver to feel comfortable making a decision or assisting. A family caregiver may be a person who has never had to make significant decisions and is now having to make them for a person who may have never been sick or had any major illness before. We see guilt, dependency, sibling dynamics, financial threats, and cohesion injected into the caregiving situation. The ultimate goal should always be the health, well-being, and safety of the parent.[33] When exploring what is involved in being a caregiver, we do not want what to dismiss what are taboo issues in many families such as

---

[32] Neil T. Anderson and Terry E. Zuehlke, *Christ-Centered Therapy* (Grand Rapids, MI: Zondervan Publishing House, 2002), 132.

[33] Margaret A. Christenson, *Aging in the Designed Environment* (Binghamton, New York: Haworth Press, 1990), 40.

who is responsible for making decisions for a parent, who is the primary caregiver, finances, insurance, forgiveness, caregiver, and care-receiver personalities.

Financial Resources

The United States government has reported that "most older Americans live in adequate, affordable housing";[34] however, there are a significant number of older adults who live in costly, physically inadequate, crowded housing, creating serious concerns for the seniors' health and physical well-being. Some older Americans now have to budget a larger portion of their financial resources toward housing. When housing expenses comprise a relatively high proportion of total expenses, there is less money available for health care, savings, and other needed goods and services. Since the burden of housing cost is relative to expenditures, they decline as income increases. Housing costs have continued to be a concern over the years, and there is the same concern with intergenerational households. They continue to be confronted by the same housing problems such as lack of complete plumbing, multiple and major upkeep concerns, along with overcrowding in many generational households. The average that a household spent on housing for those sixty-five years and older was about 35 percent of their annual income.[35]

With these statistics in hand, it is probable that there are individuals in our congregations who could benefit from physical and financial assistance. The Church does not have to take on these needs by itself. There are other organizations that might specialize in the area of need in which an individual or family requires assistance. By knowing of and locating resources for others, this allows the Church to supply support in other areas without duplicating the services of other organizations. The Church's involvement might be something as simple as helping the

---

[34]   United States Government, "Older Americans 2016 Key Indicators of Well-Being."

[35]   Ibid.

individual set up an appointment or getting them transportation to an appointment. There are numerous ways in which the Church can help the elderly that cost nothing or relatively little.

Until recently many older Americans had retired from full-time work, or had planned to do so. Because of recent economic downturns and financial depression in the mid-2000s to 2015, many semiretired and retired individuals had to return to work, or to help out family members who were affected by the depression. Some older adults cashed in their retirements, others returned to work due to loss of investments, while still others shared living residence with their children to help assist each other financially. When Social Security was initially introduced, it was designed to supplement an individual's pension and other income from assets. Currently Social Security has taken on greater importance and is the primary source of income for many Americans. While an individual is still investigating the possibility of being a caregiver, he should be sure to know what his parent's financial situation is like. Some areas that such a person might want to investigate further are:

1. Do the parents receive any checks such as retirement, Social Security, or an annuity payment? If so, how much and how often are these checks scheduled to be sent to the parent?
2. Do the parents own their residence, or pay rent? If the latter, then how much per month?
3. What other expenditures such as utilities, insurance, and cable television do they have?
4. Do they have any savings or investments?
5. Are their finances in the negative, neutral, or no concerns?
6. What type of alternate housing will they be able to afford? Is the care receiver willing to pay for the housing, or do they expect you or other family members to pay for the housing?

Social Security

The Social Security program has provided the largest share of income for older Americans since the 1960s. Social Security accounted for 49 percent per capita family income on an average for those sixty-five years and older. The share of all other income resources, pensions, and earnings have declined over the last ten years, while income from assets has also decreased.[36] In "Boomers Prefer Aging at Home," Gelhaus noted that "...a MetLife Mature Market Institute poll found that a majority of the Baby Boomers believe they are not going to need ongoing health care during their retirement years."[37] Baby boomers think they will not have a need for making financial provisions for long-term care, according to the survey. The survey results showed that 79 percent have little or no concern regarding having enough money to live in their retirement years comfortably and 62 percent planned to use Medicare to pay for long-term care services. Another 40 percent expect to use health insurance, a misconception about what funding sources are available for this type of care. Gelhaus concluded, "This study shows that Americans need to think realistically about their health and mortality. They also need to be better informed about their retirement living and long-term care options in retirement so that they can make the right decisions about their needs."[38] Unless the parent brings up finances, this can be a difficult but very important subject to approach. It is important for the parent to have a caregiver, executor, a child, or a trusted individual to know that the individual is making responsible decisions about their finances. By having someone to oversee their finances, this helps ensure that bills are paid, and that the parent is making sound decisions. There is nothing worse than to discover that your loved one has been scammed out of their life savings, property, or cash, and they are left broke and penniless. At this point, when and if the person realizes they have been scammed, they are

---

[36] Ibid.

[37] L. Gelhaus, "Boomers Prefer Aging at Home," *Provider Magazine* 30 (2004), 12–15.

[38] Ibid.

usually too embarrassed or waited too long to tell anyone, so very little, if anything, can be done. When discussing these subjects, it is best to tell one's parent it is like having an accident insurance policy. You do not expect to use it, but when you fall and hurt your back, it is sure comforting to know that you have an accident policy. It is comforting to know that there is someone to review expenses regularly to be sure that there are no financial irregularities.

Medicare

The Medicare program is a health insurance for the disabled and aged. The program is administered by the Center for Medicare and Medicaid Services. Medicare Part A is provided free to those who qualify and receive Social Security payments. The program consists of two parts, A and B. Part A provides coverage for the cost by eligible beneficiaries for inpatient hospital care, inpatient care in a nursing facility following a hospital stay, home health care, and hospice services. Each of the services has specific conditions that must be met before Medicare services are provided.[39] Medicare Part B is a voluntary program that eligible beneficiaries who pay a monthly premium are entitled to have physicians and other medical service providers reimbursed. Medicare will not pay for care that is primarily custodial. Some areas that an individual will want to investigate are:

1. Is your parent eligible for Medicare?
2. If your parent is eligible for Medicare, have they signed up?
3. Talk to a Medicare representative to determine what is covered by this insurance. What is not covered by this insurance? What alternatives are available?

---

[39] Ruth Davis, *The Nursing Home Handbook* (Holbrook, MA: Adams Media Corporation, 2000), 47.

Medicaid

The Medicaid program is administered by each state and is designed for the disabled and low income. Each state has their specific requirements for acceptance into the program. Married patients can expect the income from individuals, and their combined assets will be considered in determining Medicaid eligibility. The maximum amount that is allowed to support the remaining spouse at home varies from state to state. A person is required to use a significant portion of their assets to meet their expenses before payment proceeds. Knowing what the program rules are for Medicaid and Medicare can be very beneficial to an individual and family, and can be achieved by making an appointment with a Medicare specialist and an elder-care attorney. If a parent does not go with a child, then the child should do this alone so that he understands what the rules of the programs are. The Medicare, Social Security, and Medicaid representatives should be able to provide information to give to the parent to read and discuss at a later date. Remind the parents that this discussion is not about a child trying to find out how much money that they have, but it is more about helping them protect their assets. Because program rules can change, it is more prudent and beneficial to contact the outside resources for updated information than read outdated information.

Trying to Be Better Than Those before Us

It is not as easy as it looks. Growing up, most children think that they can do a better job than their parents are doing. But when one marries and has children of his own, the realities of life start rearing their ugly heads. He begins to reevaluate those parenting ideals and starts to understand some of the decisions that his parents made while he was growing up. We are commanded in Exodus 20:12 to "honor" our father and mother and "obey them" in Ephesians 6:1. In the following excerpt, William Carl reminded us that God did not ask or present us with the option to only honor our parents if they were loving, good, and kind:

So, we have a commandment: "Honor your father and your mother." Still more deeply, the commandment addresses the progression of human beings across the sweep of time, generation after generation. My grandparents were served by my parents, and my parents served by me, and, in turn, I may be served by my children, and they in turn by their children. Our parents may have been wicked, almost as wicked as we are with our children, but, nonetheless, they are our parents and they have given us birth before God. The fact is that our aging parents will soon be replaced by aging us. Even as we may hope for patience and affection in our gray-headed years, so we seek to honor our father and mother. The commandment displays a kind of tenderness toward our common time swept humanity. In so doing it calls for a certain civility between the generations, and not only civility but mercy. Good heavens, we are all bad parents, no matter how many courses in parenting we digest; we are all without exception sin-struck parents who damage our children. So, as sinners, who are the children of sinners, and who in turn breed sinners, we cling to the shape of human courtesy which, in a way, is the next best thing to love. We honor our fathers and mothers and hope that our days will be long in the land God has given us.[40]

Even though the times have changed, maybe those childhood days were not as bad as we thought. We can only go with what we have seen, lived, and been taught. As parents we will each have our own family and life experiences as a starting point. Maybe our initial parenting goal should be to be better in the good-skill areas our parents had and good in the bad areas. Who did our parents have as parenting role models? Did they have anyone as a role model, or were they doing the best they could with what they had at the time? Parenting has evolved just as our society continues to evolve and change. What was a new idea five years ago can be old and outdated now. Each generation brings new ideas and grows up

---

[40] David Buttrick, *Graying Gracefully: Preaching to Older Adults* (Louisville, KY: Westminster John Knox Press, 1997), 36–37.

having the distinct characteristics of that generation. It was a generation or more ago that we were children and our parents were raising us. Think about it, and pray about the possibility of enjoying the time we have left with our parents starting today.

Do I Have to Forgive that Person?

Families have problems, and in some instances they can be severe and unspeakable. The problems could be from drugs, alcohol, abuse, abandonment, or any other number of hurtful things that man does to another. Once someone has broken or lost our trust, giving forgiveness seems impossible. In most instances, our initial feeling is that we will never be able to trust or forgive them again. Trust and forgiveness are two of the hardest things for us to give back to another individual. How many millions of people alive today are trapped and in bondage to bitterness and resentments because of their lack of desire to pray for and work toward forgiving life's hurts? To err is human; to forgive is divine. One individual stated that he was so bitter that if you could lick his heart, it would poison you. Once he began to forgive the other person, a burden was lifted off him, and he was able to go on and live a life as God has designed for him. Remember that the forgiveness of a hurt can take time, along with effort and prayer and sometimes the help of a counselor. Forgiveness is not a wimp response to a hurt. It does not mean excusing or minimalizing a hurt. Do not confuse the gospel call to forgive over and over with toleration of ongoing hurtful behavior. The Christian call to forgive does not mean that we tolerate ongoing abuse from someone.

Actions that Speak Louder Than Words

Not everyone has good parents or fond childhood memories. I am reminded of such a story from a coworker one day as we were talking about where we lived during our childhood. We had both grown up in colder Midwestern states, and we were now glad to be living in the warmer south. I was caught off guard by what he shared next. He said,

"My mother was a terrible mom, and she has been married eight times. I have three siblings, one who is still living and the other committed suicide." He went on to explain that his dad was his mother's third husband, and he learned to hate his dad and his stepmother because of all of the lies his mother told him as a young child. He eventually went to live with his dad because of the circumstances at home with his mother when he was entering middle school. This was when he started discovering the lies his mother had told him and his brothers over the years.

He talks fondly of his father today, and the relationship they have was built over the years. When asked about his mother he said, "The more I learned how dishonest she had been and the type of person that she was, our contact became almost nothing over the years. There was just a call now and then to say hello. Unexpectedly I received a call one day from my mother's neighbor whom I did not know. They informed me that they could no longer help her because her Alzheimer's had gotten too bad and she was very combative." My friend went on to explain that this was news to him because she seemed okay whenever they talked on the telephone. "Now what?" he thought. His mother lived about two thousand miles away, and they wanted him there now, or they were going to call adult protective services. He made arrangements to leave the next morning and drive to where his mother was living.

When he arrived, he was blown away by the poor living conditions and wondered why someone had not called sooner. On the drive down, he'd had a lot of time to think. His brother had made it clear in a phone call that he was not going to get involved, and in fact this brother had not spoken to their mother in almost twenty years. During the drive and the days that followed it, my coworker said he had to "...deeply search his soul and make a choice. [He] was either going to have to walk away from the situation or forgive [his] mother." He decided to forgive his mother and bring her back to his home and be the primary caregiver. He did not know what else to do; there was no one else available, as she had alienated everyone rather severely. He went on to say, "There were endless amounts of paperwork and telephone calls to make; this all happened in a few days." He packed up her belongings in his car and off they went.

The roles were now reversed: he was the caregiver, and she was the care receiver. He explained, "Forgiveness did not change the fact that she was a terrible mother and at times a worse person. I had to forgive her for me so that I could move on in life and not be hindered and drug [sic] down by my anger and resentment. It was not easy some days, but it was the right thing to do. Life is better now." She lived with him until her Alzheimer's progressed, and he was not able to care for her anymore. He found a care facility that has twenty-four-hour care.

Currently he visits her regularly and takes her out for lunch several Sundays per month. Family dynamics are sticky. There is so much history, hurt, and lost time involved in each family situation. My friend has alluded that his childhood was less than perfect but that he had made a conscious decision to move forward. He chose to honor his mother and be her caregiver. Is their relationship perfect? No, but it did get better, and he said that in her own way, "She did apologize for what she had done before her Alzheimer's got worse." Did he have to do this? Would anyone who knew his story have blamed him if he had said no? We each have our own story, and we can choose to ignore the Holy Spirit or follow His lead. In this story, he felt led to care for his mother. Another person's story might be completely different; of course, that is why it is another person's story.

Why Forgiveness

1. Because Jesus tells us to, saying, "If you forgive those who sin against you, your heavenly Father will forgive you. But if you refuse to forgive others, your Father will not forgive your sins" (Matthew 6:14–15).
2. To free us physically. Forgiveness can free us physically from migraines, stress, back strain, and stomach problems. These are just a few of the health problems that can occur as stated in the

book *None of these Diseases*.[41] Lack of forgiveness can lead to relentless physical and mental pain and issues.

3. To restore peace. When we promote forgiveness, we start getting the benefits of peace in our homes and family. We get rid of that negative energy that you can feel and the thick air that can be cut with a knife.

How do we get to forgiveness? We get there by prayer. Prayer is an important discipline. Our prayers should not be a matter of duty, but of joy and expectation. Prayer should be something we look forward to doing. Our prayers and earnestness should cultivate intimacy with God so that we look forward to hearing from Him. We should look forward to our time with God. This time should leave us refreshed and stress free, even when His answer is no. Do you remember that He has your best interest at heart and He has got this?

There is one thing that we all have in common: we are all going to get old. Do we want to get old burdened by a lack of forgiveness? Some people need help with forgiveness whether it be a parent, caregiver, or friend. At times people need help in learning how to give forgiveness and receive it. Lifting the burden that a lack of forgiveness brings can make a significant difference in an individual's life. If you know someone who is having trouble with forgiveness or you yourself are, it is important to seek out help. You might have a parent or friend who you believe needs help with forgiveness and recommending them to a qualified individual, and doing so could be a life changer for them and you as the caregiver. Find a trusted friend, pastor, or Christian counselor to lead your loved one down the path toward forgiveness. Forgiveness is such a critical component in the life of a caregiver, care receiver, and family members. Many decisions will have to be made while determining how much influence past personal hurts, anger, and reluctance to forgive will impact a current decision. In no manner are these writings trying to downplay the events that might

---

[41]   S. I. McMillen, *None of These Diseases* (Grand Rapids, MI: Spire Books, 1963).

have caused these personal feelings. What the reader should be aware of is that the absence of forgiveness can play a central part in the decisions a caregiver will have to make.

Chapter Highlights

As we are now discovering, caregiving is not for the slow moving and faint of heart. A caregiver can be in constant motion because of all the components, decisions, and involvement of others. We can feel like a hamster on a wheel trying to get information, but it feels like we are not making any headway. In this chapter we have discussed being a better caregiver than those before us, learning that there is no blueprint to caregiving because each person and family have unique health concerns, culture, financial responsibilities, and personalities. We are commanded to honor our father and mother, and this can be difficult for both the caregiver and care receiver because of negative past histories. As hard as it can be, forgiving others and letting go can have a positive spiritual impact on us and on others.

A person may have already taken on the role of caregiver, but there is nothing that says they must do this forever. Another individual may have abruptly made the decision to bring their parent into their home, discovering only three months later that the situation is not working at all. It is permissible to change one's mind. One should pray and go where God is leading them. One can still honor one's parent even if they have to admit them into a nursing home; honoring one's parent is not necessarily having the parent move into one's home. One can honor his parents when one visits them in the nursing home regularly, by calling them on the phone, or by bringing them their favorite snack when visiting. Honoring one's parent is being respectful and helping to meet their needs. There is no specific list of requirements telling us what honoring a parent is. For one child, it might be to do repairs around the parent's house or purchase groceries for them if they are having financial difficulties. The way in which one can honor their parents is only limited by their desire to help. One should not let his emotions make decisions for them, as doing so when making caregiver decisions can lead to disastrous results.

Before starting the next chapter, be sure to read the next section, "Purposeful Talk and Thought through Questions." Take a few minutes to think about your answers. If you are studying this book with other individuals, listen to their experiences, answers, and ideas. Can you use any of this information and apply it to your situation to have a better outcome? Is it possible that you might need to make some changes in past caregiving decisions because circumstances have changed? Being a caregiver requires a person to turn on a dime many times. We are dealing with an aging person whose health circumstances are always changing.

Purposeful Thought and Talk through Questions

Here is an opportunity to go deeper into the chapter. By using the discussion questions below, you have an opportunity through self-talk, counseling, or a small group session to discuss scenarios and to think about different options through engaging in conversation. These questions are not designed to be controversial or divisive. There are no right or wrong answers, as each individual and family have different life situations and experiences.

1. Have you discussed alternative housing with your parents or for yourself in the event you are not able to live at home alone safely? Why, or why not?
2. How has your perception of caregiving changed from when you began reading this book?
3. What advantages can you see from checking into rules that govern Medicare and Social Security?
4. Have you discussed general finances with your parents, or your children for yourself?
5. Do you believe there are any issues in your family regarding reluctance to forgive that could benefit from prayer and assistance from a pastor or a counselor?

CHAPTER 3

The Physical, Mental, and Emotional Aspects of Caregiving

"Two are better than one, because they have a good return for their labor: If either of them falls down, one can help the other up. But pity anyone who falls and has no one to help them up. Also, if two lie down together, they will keep warm. But how can one keep warm lone? Though one may be overpowered, two can defend themselves. A cord of three strands is not quickly broken"

(ECCLESIASTICS 4:9–12)

Being a Caregiver Has Responsibilities

Nora was a go-getter. She was bubbly, energetic, and always helping to get things done. So it was a no-brainer that she should be the one to take care of Mom. Everyone lived an equal distance apart so Mom could just come live with her, and everyone else could visit or get her for a few days as they liked. Everyone agreed, especially Mom. She would not be so lonely now with Nora's family around, and she did need help with some things, so the idea sounded great. Whenever one of the siblings Julie or Ashley asked if Nora needed help or a break, she would always tell them no. As time went on they asked less and less, because she said everything was good. Little by little mother got sicker, and her health deteriorated, and she was able to do less and less for herself. Nora was running around now, bathing her mother, getting her mother out of bed and cooking her meals, going to the pharmacy to get her prescriptions, taking her to the doctor, and doing anything else she needed.

In most instances when Nora left the house, she would have to take her mother and the wheelchair with her, because there was no one at home to watch her. Nora also had two children and a husband who she tried to support, but she was not doing a good job of it. Now three years later Nora was feeling exhausted all of the time, had headaches, and rarely wanted to leave the house. Her husband and kids would invite her to do things, but she always refused because she was tired and just did not have any interest in anything. Nora's husband finally talked her into going to the doctor for a checkup. After a few tests and some discussions with Nora and her husband, the doctor said, "You are suffering from burnout. You have the classic symptoms. The good thing is we can treat this and get you healthy again if you listen. If you don't listen to my advice or follow the treatment plan, you will more than likely get sicker and possibly have a stroke."

Getting to the Nuts and Bolts of Caregiving

We are now getting more personal with our exploration of caregiving, such as the different types of personalities involved, the caregiver's health, caregiver stress, and burnout.

Deciding to be a caregiver is not an easy decision, nor do one's choices move in a linear direction. As we have discussed previously, this is a decision that should not be made based on emotions, but on facts. Making a decision to be a caregiver and move a parent into one's home can have a rippling effect, as it did with Nora. The harm done physically and psychologically can have long-term effects and detriments to all of those involved. The older population has grown more diverse as the population grows. This statistic reflects the demographic changes in the U.S. population as a whole over the last several decades. Programs and services for older Americans in 2060 will require greater flexibility to meet the needs of a more diverse population.[42] What better time than now for the Church to start partnering, implementing, and developing aging and caregiving programs for their community?

Know the Different Cultures in Your Community

The understanding of cultural factors is consequential to the Church and vital to effective ministry intervention. The Church will need to have an understanding of the culture where they intend to serve. If the Church does not know the population census and the culture of those in their community, it will be very puzzling how to reach and serve the people in their congregation and community. In *Functional Performance in Older Adults*, Bonder and Wagner noted, "Culture shapes attitudes and actions requiring understanding of roles and activities of older adults in a particular culture, attitudes about aging, and the way in which older individuals are valued by culture."[43] These factors are mediated by:

- the sophistication of the culture,
- the changes in a culture over time,
- the degree to which the culture settles in a specific place, and
- the demographic factors, such as the proportion of older versus younger individuals.[44]

---

[42] United States Government, "Older Americans 2016 Key Indicators of Well-Being," U.S. Government Printing Office, August 2016, accessed December 1, 2017, https://agingstats.gov/docs/LatestReport/Older-Americans-2016-Key-Indicators-of-WellBeing.pdf.

[43] Bette R. Bonder and Marilyn B. Wagner, *Functional Performance in Older Adults* (Philadelphia, PA: F. A. Davis Company, 1994), 16.

[44] Ibid.

These are some of the points that influence us as we make decisions in life. Many times we do not realize how our culture has influenced our decisions. There is a considerable difference among and between ethnic groups in the use of formal support services. Examples of cultural differences in a community might be having Vietnamese immigrants who are less likely to use formal support services and Russian immigrants who are more likely to use such services in the community. The reason for this difference is theorized by Mayerhoff that the use of services by elderly Russian immigrants is because they live a greater distance from their families and feel somewhat abandoned by them.[45] If we have an understanding of the people and their culture, then we will be better able to serve and evangelize them. If the Church feels that they need additional census information, the website www.census.gov is free and has a significant amount of information that can be applied to any area. There are also businesses that will do a customized demographic study, interpret, and explain the results to the Church leadership for a fee.

Culture is the framework that guides and binds life practices. According to Anderson and Fenichel, "The cultural framework must be viewed as a set of tendencies of policies from which to choose."[46] Cultural communities are made up of individuals, all of whom contribute their own unique characteristics to the sense of place in which they live. Differing cultures each have a different meaning or understanding of disabling and at-risk conditions. Each culture handles aging and disability situations in a different manner. The religious and medical communities could benefit if they were trained to meet the needs and to work closely with different cultures. This type of knowledge and awareness of their values and family heritage can be valuable for both parties when health conditions and options are discussed.

Some cultures encourage families to live together generation after generation, with each individual and their family remaining in the same

---

[45] Ibid., 10.

[46] Eleanor W. Lynch, Marci J. Hanson, *Developing Cross-Cultural Competence* (Baltimore, MD: Paul H. Brookes Publishing Company, 1992), 3.

household, while other cultures encourage independence, so the children leave home when they become eighteen. This leaves the parents living alone in the household in their twilight years, when they are most susceptible to needing help. This cultural account can explain the feeling that some people have toward other groups or why the impression that is left is a negative one. This does not mean that the individual or family members are not close. What is happening is that they are following a cultural script that may be good or bad without knowing why.

Types of Caregiving

In many instances, an individual's knowledge about caregiving begins with their initiation into being a caregiver unexpectedly. They do not have a reference point or a clear, unbiased understanding of the situation, or a network of support and assistance that will be essential. When family members become caregivers, they need to realize that they are going to need help and assistance. We would be wise to apply the words from Ecclesiastes 4:9–12: "Two are better than one, because they have a good return for their labor: If either of them falls down, one can help the other up. But pity anyone who falls and has no one to help them up. Also, if two lie down together, they will keep warm. But how can one keep warm alone? Though one may be overpowered, two can defend themselves. A cord of three strands is not quickly broken." Even though the verse is not directly speaking about being a caregiver, it could be. It is foolish and unwise to take on the role of a caregiver by oneself. It is a recipe for disaster without help. No man can do it all by himself without suffering the consequences physically and emotionally. We should be setting up a network before they begin the initial caring for the individual. We should be looking for:

- o   Respite care so they can take a regular break.
- o   Help to assist with daily task and activities.
- o   A support group so that they can share ideas, stories, and resources.

o   Knowledgeable professionals who the caregiver can call to ask questions and seek guidance if needed.

o   A setup for a caregiver schedule with a paid caregiver agency, or family members and volunteers. If possible, try to keep the days the same each week and month. When the dates become regular and familiar, then an individual will know to plan their activities for another day. This helps keep from conflict developing, and the caregiving will not fall upon one individual or family.

Caregiving in the home is generally provided by one of two groups: hired professionals, or family and friends.

1. Employed professional caregivers: *Home care* and *home health* are two separate types of care that are both provided in a home setting. Many individuals and families do not know that there are differences between these two terms and mistakenly use them interchangeably. The primary difference is that home care is non-clinical care, and home health is clinical care. Home-health services can include:

   • Therapy and skilled nursing services
   • Administration of medications, including injections
   • Medical tests
   • Monitoring of health status
   • Wound care

   Home-care services provided by home-care aides may include:

   • Meal preparation
   • House cleaning
   • Helping with dressing, bathing, and grooming
   • Transportation

- Reminders to take medicine
- Help with bill paying

There is nothing wrong with using both services. Some families have found the need to use these services after a hospitalization. The home-health staff addresses the clinical and rehabilitative needs of the parent during the transition home. During this same time period, a home-care aide can help with personal caregiving and household chores that the parent requires assistance with during their recovery. Finding help is not always easy. It is better to look for services before they are needed. The services that one requests initially will change as one's parent's health changes. There will be a change in the need for more caregiver-assistance time and possibly an additional caregiver will be needed at a fixed time of the day, such as for personal hygiene or traveling to medical appointments. There are several things that should be done before hiring a caregiver or health-care agency. Whether one hires an individual or an agency, there are some fundamental questions that one should address before hiring anyone:

a. Decide what task and activities that one wants the caregiver to provide.
b. Develop a job description so that everyone knows what the expectations are.
c. Ask for references and call to check them out.
d. Explain the expectations to the caregiver.
e. Ask about the agency's procedure for reporting if a task is completed incorrectly or not at all.
f. Find out what type of services they provide.
g. Keep the line of communications open.
h. Tell them about the parent; even the most experienced caregiver needs basic information about the client. They need to know the client's food likes and dislikes, medication schedule, daily schedule, and contact numbers.

2. Family members or friends as caregivers: Our society today is very mobile, and individuals and families move on the average every five years until retirement.[47] In many instances, family members become long-distance caregivers because they are not able to move into the individual's residence or to the vicinity where the elderly individual lives due to employment, children, and financial limitations. A family member can act as a long-distance caregiver and still live in the vicinity. What the long-distance caregiver can do is hire a part-time caregiver and ask a friend or neighbor to check in on the resident to see how they are doing and provide assistance as needed. The family member is still making all of the decisions except they are having a local caregiver inform them of how the elderly individual is progressing. The long-distance caregiver can also visit the family member during the week, on the weekends, for a few visits a month. The visits will let the caregiver get a visual of how their loved one is doing and help them decide if this is still a safe living arrangement. This type of caregiving is for the individual who needs minimal assistance and can be left home alone safely during the day. When the individual can no longer be left home alone safely, then other housing options will need to be explored.

There is another alternative that is a combination of several different alternatives. If an individual is not sure of what to do, feels uncomfortable making this decision alone, lives out of the area, or is constrained by time, then hiring a geriatric-care manager could be beneficial. A geriatric-care manager is a nurse or social worker who is trained to work under difficult and trying circumstances. Their mission is to advocate for the care of the elderly individual by developing a care plan that considers the individual's health, quality of life issues, and financial status. A case manager will assess the individual and make recommendations concerning what type

---

[47]   U.S., United States Census Bureau, accessed May 1, 2017, https://www.census.gov/prod/2014pubs/p20-574.pdf.

of help is needed, as well as safety measures and area agencies that supply services and equipment that are in the best interest of the parent. This is not a free service, so before hiring a geriatric-care manager or anyone else, one should ask for a reference and have a background check completed. If one is hiring a company to supply the geriatric-care manager, ask for their references and if they do background checks on their employees. Be cautious; it is important to be comfortable with the individual or company and their skills before hiring them. They will be a conduit for information and decision making, so it is imperative that they are competent at their job and that the information they provide can be trusted.

Is This Job for Me?

It is essential that one is honest with oneself if one is going to be a caregiver. Before the discussion of having enough help and where the care recipient will live, a conversation about emotional well-being and personalities has to take place. These can be tough questions to answer because they can carry old animosities and wounds that we thought were buried or might not want to face. Some of the questions that will need to be answered are:

a. Are there any unresolved resentment and anger between the caregiver and care receiver?

b. Can the caregiver and care receiver get along with one another, as well as with other members of the caregiver's family, seven days a week?

c. Even with help can the caregiver meet the care receiver's demands? Is the care receiver a demanding person?

d. Is the potential caregiver willing to give up his privacy and that of his family's, in his own home with the parent living there and with other caregivers coming and going?

e. Can the caregiver ignore the attitudes, actions, and words from the care receiver? Such as, "Your sister does that better," "Why

can't you get this right?" "I don't like being here," or "Why are
you doing this to me?" This is a sampling of some of the remarks
that could be made and inevitably at a time one least expects it.

The mental stress of being a caregiver is equally important and just as
stressful as the physical stress. There is the possibility that it would not be
in the best interest of either party for a particular individual to be the primary caregiver because of revolving personal issues. An individual might
have enough room in their house, their family is in agreement, and they
do not have to work for financial reasons. One hindrance or drawback
might be that the caregiver and parent never could get along comfortably.
In the past, it was hard for there to be peace for more than a few hours
before something was said by the parent or child, and the other one got
mad and stormed out of the house. Is it wise to think this relationship will
change? Is there a problem that no one has been willing to address over
the years? Could it be that the two have such different personalities and
have not learned how to accept the other person's personality? These are
the questions that one has to answer before even beginning the caregiving
process and involving others. The individual must be honest and recognize that this might be a situation where they should not be a caregiver.

There is nothing wrong or sinful with making such a decision. There
are numerous other ways in which a person can help and be involved in
the parent's life positively. This might be the time when the individual
starts looking at other feasible options. If one thinks they can work with
their parent but there is a personality challenge, they might try speaking
with a counselor or pastor and see if they can give some insight on how
to harmonize their personality with that of their parent. Whether these
are personal or not, it could be encouraging and insightful to take one of
the personality tests to help the caregivers determine innovative ways to
react to the parent's personality type. One of the things that the potential
caregiver and other family members can discuss are temperament and
personality analyses, which can provide information as to how an individual will react in different situations. With this information, one can

learn to predict the behavioral characteristics of how one's parent will probably react to different situations and circumstances. Another advantage to having this information about different personality types is that it can help an individual prepare for a variety of responses so that they are not caught off guard as a caregiver. This is where an experienced Christian counselor or pastor can be a benefit, because they can provide information and guidance on aging issues, personalities, temperaments, and the process involved in elder-care cognitive issues. The counselor will also be able to explain the different options, provide information, and help those involved develop strategies based on the personalities of the caregivers.

The idea of temperament theory itself has a long history and goes back some 2,500 years.

Temperament theory is an option to learning more about the different personal characteristics and can be explained in the counselor's office in a relatively quick manner. The personality profile can be taken and test results scored in a few minutes. After the personality characteristics are determined, they can be adapted to the caregiving circumstances. Researchers over the years have studied temperament theory and categorized temperament theory into four basic temperament types: sanguine, melancholy, choleric, and phlegmatic. Knowing the personality types of those involved can give insight into how such individuals will react to various circumstances and decisions that are made and will have to be made. Below is the list of personality characteristics, including their general strengths and weaknesses:

- Sanguine
    - Strengths: talkative, outgoing, warm, enthusiastic, personable, friendly, compassionate, carefree
    - Weaknesses: weak-willed, unstable, restless, undependable, egocentric, loud, exaggerates, fearful

- Melancholy
  - Strengths: gifted, analytical, sensitive, perfectionist, aesthetic, idealistic, loyal
  - Weaknesses: self-centered, moody, negative, theoretical, impractical, unsociable, critical

- Choleric
  - Strengths: strong-willed, determined, independent, optimistic, practical, productive, leader
  - Weaknesses: crafty, unemotional, proud, angry, cruel, sarcastic, domineering, inconsiderate

- Phlegmatic
  - Strengths: calm, easy-going, dependable, efficient, conservative, diplomatic, practical
  - Weaknesses: stingy, fearful, indecisive, spectator, unmotivated, self-productive, selfish[48]

Even though we are not purely one personality or the other but a mix, we can still come to a probable conclusion as to which temperaments will have a more difficult time of accepting an illness, declining health, or a change in living arrangements. The sanguine and phlegmatic temperaments are more likely to accept a change in residence or serious illness. The choleric and melancholy individual would have a more difficult time adjusting to or accepting their situation, and would work hard to change it even if they knew it was unchangeable. When discussing personality characteristics, it is important to remember that we are not one personality or the other; we are a blended personality. The blended personality is the mixing cohesively together of personalities or temperaments. Since we are usually more than one temperament, if the strengths of each are used properly and the weaknesses de-magnified, the outcome can be positive. We cannot make a person over or redesign them, but we can pray

---

[48] Florence Littauer, *Your Personality Tree* (Waco, TX: Word Books, 1986), 79.

for them. Everyone is slightly irregular and different from each other, even those with the same temperament classifications.

Another tool that might be useful is a generational differences chart. A generational differences chart will list what a particular generation's feeling are toward different categories, such as work, finances, or health. The information summarizes the personality characteristics and beliefs of many individuals in that generation. This information should not be used as an absolute guide, nor should any of the other tools that have been mentioned or presented. These tools are presented to assist in trying to understand the behavior of a parent and to increase positive communication with them. There is an example of a generational chart at the end of the chapter. One important thing to keep in mind is that some medications, illnesses, and diseases will cause a person to act in a manner that might be abnormal relative to their regular personality.

This is a time to be uniting together, being and thinking Christlike. When individuals of different temperaments are working together effectively and using the strengths and weaknesses of each other, they can produce the most positive outcomes possible. It is acceptable to be different in a positive way, meaning that we do not all need to be the same temperament to get along. We can blend together and be effective for the cause of Christ by remembering that we are all different temperament-wise, but serve the same risen Savior.

Caregivers and Burnout

In "Family Caregiving of the Elderly Parent," Vicki Moore Northern stated, "Caregiver burden is a term that refers to the managing of specific task needed to be done for the care receiver. Caregiver stress, on the other hand, refers to the subjective feelings of strain on the caregiver."[49] If these things are not managed properly, they can lead to burnout. Burnout is very prevalent when an individual becomes a caregiver, and it

---

[49] Vicki Moore Northern, "Family Caregiving of the Elderly Parent," *Journal of Family Ministry* 16, no. 1 (Spring 2002), 43.

does not matter whether one is a family member or a health-care professional. As counselors, caregiver assistance should be one of the first topics we discuss with our counselee because no one is immune from burnout and its effects. Almost everyone is prone to it, some more than others. It can sneak up on an individual without him even being aware that it has happened.

Burnout is a phrase used to describe a feeling of physical and emotional exhaustion that-comes after we have had prolonged involvement with people and work situations that demand our time, energy, and strength. In the past, the term "burnout" was used to describe counselors and other professionals who were people helpers and had become tense, discouraged, and overwhelmed by the demands of working intensively and for hours with people in need. Recently it has become apparent that counselors are not the only ones who experience burnout. Nurses, lawyers, physicians, sales people, business executives, and parents are among those who experience periodic burnout. In days gone by, the term burnout was made about a game of catch in which the ball was thrown progressively harder each time until one player's hand is stinging from the hard, fast throws, and they will quit right then. That is how a caregiver who does not take care of themselves can feel: anxious, overwhelmed, hurting, and ready to give up now.

The term burnout has become a catchall phrase for other unrelated situations, and as such the severity of the situation and the meaning of the word has been lost and deflated the burnout-syndrome meaning. It is not easy for those in the helping professions to interact intensely and continually with people who demand a lot, who are hurting or under pressure. Care receivers demand a lot of their time, energy, and concentration, and they are unable to give very much in return. In many instances, those in the helping professions feel for and with them. If they hurt, we hurt; if they are sad, we are sad. One of the most intensive studies on burnout was done at the University of California in Berkeley. Researchers discovered that there are several signs that indicated an individual was developing burnout. Some of the behavior characteristics and indicators are:

- detaching from other people by staying at home, spending less time with others, being aloof, cynical, less involved emotionally;
- beginning to run down physically and having frequent headaches, fatigue, loss of physical energy, high blood pressure, cramps, sleeplessness, arthritis, ulcers, and spasms; and
- influenced psychologically by low morale, forgetfulness, self-condemnation, and "what's the use" attitude prevails.[50]

Many times, when an individual begins experiencing burnout symptoms, they do not have the slightest idea what is going on within their body. They might start trying to overcome problems by working harder, taking medications that mask the problems, or trying to ignore the uneasy feeling and keep the same caregiving schedule. Burnout symptoms only increase the frustration, and in many instances the caregiver will take out their frustration and fatigue on their family, the care receiver, and themselves; those are the ones to suffer. Some caregivers will change employers only to repeat the same cycle, and some will even get fired from their jobs. How does one break the cycle of burnout? As a caregiver, one faces many of the same dilemmas that professional caregivers can face. So is one a candidate for burnout? The medical sciences have discovered that different types of personalities can be predisposed to different medical problems under stress.

Are You More Prone to Burnout?

Which personalities are more prone to burnout and stress-related illnesses? The Type A (melancholy, choleric) personality is more prone to burnout than the Type B (phlegmatic, sanguine) personality. The Type A person is highly competitive, feels the pressure of time, and may react to frustration with hostility. The Type A person is more likely to set

---

deadlines or quotas for himself at work or home at least once a week. The Type A person brings his work home frequently. This type of person is highly achievement oriented and pushes himself to near capacity. Some behaviorists say that the Type A person earns the rewards they seek, but it may come at perhaps at the cost of their health. The Type A individual is at a greater risk for heart attack when under stress than the Type B individual. Along with the risk of heart attack, there is also the possibility of migraines, tension headaches, asthma, colitis, backaches, and an array of other physical maladies.

The Type B personality puts in his time at work and seldom brings his work home. His interest is more in sports and leisure-time activities. He is not a slave to time, and proving his worth to himself or others is not a strong requirement of his personality. He has the ability to be as intelligent as the Type A personality, but he does not work at it. The Type B personality is less likely to demand strong control of his life or environment.[51] He goes with the flow and does not fight the upstream battle like the salmon. How to cope in many instances is easier said than done. We humans like to be able to control our own fates. One of the main things that increase stress is the feeling of the loss of control. If one accepted the fact that he cannot and is not able to control all events, he would be in a much better position to start managing stress. Stress is what is usually accompanied by feelings of arousal and agitation. When a person is undergoing stress, they feel keyed-up, and the problems become more evident when such arousals occur, and actions become more primitive.

A caregiver can avoid burnout with proper coping techniques. There are successful coping strategies that work, and one can overcome the situation and practice the stress-relief strategies when needed. When an individual sees themselves as passive and their future controlled by others, they are more susceptible to stress. If an individual has a self-concept of a more active nature, they are less susceptible to stress. If one can

---

[51] Saul McLeod, "Type A Personality," 2017, accessed August 1, 2017, https://www.simplypsychology.org/ personality-a.html.

learn to think of themselves in dynamic rather than static terms, they might be more resistant to stress. One should get away from the labeling of every situation as stressful and never-ending, which creates a thinking pattern of hopelessness and despair. These feelings give the individual the perception that the stress will go on forever. The stress can be painful and disabling because their perception is that it will never end. One's stubbornness to take care of themselves physically and mentally can end either in burnout or worse, if one does not cognitively take care of oneself.

Strategies for Reducing Caregiver Distress

Some of the strategies that have proven successful are:

- <u>The need for time alone</u>. Take short rest breaks throughout the day and a few days' vacation from the office, kids, and in-laws.
- <u>Shared responsibilities</u>. Train others to help with tasks that do not require a specific individual to complete them. If one can remember that they cannot do it all, they will be healthier and happier.
- <u>Group support</u>. By networking with other caregivers and professionals, one can get their support, ideas, and resources.
- <u>Proper exercise and diet</u>. A nutritious diet and active lifestyle can aid in reduction of stress through toning up the body, relieving tension, and getting energy and strength through a proper diet and exercise.
- <u>Assertiveness</u>. Learning to say no when one has too much on their plate, even when the request is simple and easy to do. A polite "no" with a short statement that one is overbooked and could not give the project the proper attention would suffice.

Burnout is a common experience among caregivers because of the level of stress they are under, constantly giving to their parent who is in need. If burnout has not affected an individual yet, it can if they do not plan regular help and regular physical and mental rest periods. Burnout can be handled and conquered if we are aware of its influence and willing to tackle it head-on.

Elder Abuse Is Real

Another area in which many caregivers think that they are immune is elder abuse. As Christian counselors and pastors, we should stress the importance to every caregiver and family member who is giving the care to be mindful that no caregiver is immune from creating an abusive situation, especially when one is tired, frustrated, and stressed. Some self-checking questions:

1. Am I getting enough rest and relaxation so that I do not become angry, rough, ill-tempered, and slothful in providing care? As soon as we let these actions take hold, we are pushing the line to become an abusive caregiver.
2. Be observant of those providing care for your parent. Look to see if they are being respectful and doing their job safely. Other areas to be observant of are to check your parent to see if there are any bruises, if they are losing weight, or if their personality changed. These can be signs of possible abuse, and further investigation is probably warranted.
3. Accessing recreational and activity services can be stress relievers and relaxing for both the caregiver and care receiver. Research has shown that individuals remaining active in later life have a higher satisfaction level.[52]

Perhaps the most useful and widely accepted definition of stress is the one that is mainly attributed to Richard S. Lazarus: stress is a condition or feeling experienced when a person perceives that "demands exceed

---

[52] Federal Interagency Forum on Aging-Related Statistics, "Older Americans 2016 Key Indicators of Well-Being," August 2016, accessed December 14, 2017, http://agingstats.gov/docs/LatestReport/Older-Americans-2016-Key-Indicators-of-WellBeing.pdf.

the personal and social resources the individual is able to mobilize."[53] In less formal terms, we feel stressed when we feel that "things are out of control."[54]

Our ability to cope with the demands upon us is key to our experience of stress. For example, starting a new job might be a wholly exciting experience if everything else in one's life is stable and positive. But if one starts a new job when they have just moved into a new house or their partner is ill, or when experiencing money problems, they might find it very hard to cope.

How much of this does it take to push someone "over the edge"? Not all unusual events are equally hard to deal with or consequential. For example, compare the stress of divorce with that of a change in responsibilities at work. Because of extreme life changes, one needs to be able to rate and measure the total stress score appropriately. There are several tests that an individual can administer to themselves by answering some questions. The more honest one is when answering the questions, the more helpful the results will be. There are tests that can be completed online and scored, such as the Disc Personality Test that can be found at https://www.123test.com/disc-personality-test/. The Holmes-Rahe Life Stress Test is another test that can assist with determining whether or not one is on the path toward burnout.

The Holmes-Rahe Life Stress Inventory

The Holmes and Rahe Stress Scale, also known as the Social Readjustment Rating Scale, is a short quiz that can help determine if one is on the road to burnout. This questionnaire can be completed in a few minutes, and the rating scale is included. If after taking the quiz one's score does not rate in a risk area, but this person has been feeling tired, making an appointment to see a physician is advised. This quiz is a guide

---

53   Richard Lazarus, The Holmes and Rahe Test Scale, July 26, 2013, accessed November 10, 2017, http://slipstream6011719.wordpress.com/tag/richard-lazarus/.

54   Ibid.

and an assessment of health. To be sure that there are no other health problems, make an appointment with a physician to get a checkup and let them make the determination concerning your health.

The Social Readjustment Rating Scale (SRRS) was created to do just that. This tool helps us measure the stress load we carry and think about what we should do about it.[55] Dr. Thomas Holmes and Dr. Richard Rahe developed a study to determine whether stress contributes to illness. More than 5,000 medical patients were surveyed and asked if they had experienced any of the listed forty-three life events during the previous two years. The more events that were added up increased the individual's score. The larger the score of each event, the more likely the individual was to become ill. Each event is called a Life Change Unit (LCU), and carries a different total for the stress. This is just one of several tools available to help an individual realize that they should receive outside counsel from a physician, pastor, or Christian counselor to determine what life-adjustment changes they might benefit from making. The test is easy to take but requires the honesty of the test taker during the test and when reviewing the results.

The Social Readjustment Rating Scale

LIFE EVENT	MEAN VALUE	MY SCORE
Death of a spouse	100	
Divorce	73	
Marital separation from mate	65	
Jail term	63	
Death of close family member	63	

[55] Mind Tools Content Team, The Holmes, and Rahe Stress Scale, accessed October 25, 2017, https://www.mindtools.com/pages/article/newTCS_82.htm?utm_term=holmes+rahe+stress+scale&utm_content=p1-main-3-title&utm_medium=sem&utm_source=msn_s&utm_campaign=adid-9916ce56-9147-4f81-9ccd-8f488aa4b406-0-ab_msb_ocode-22837&ad=semD&an=msn_s&am=broad&q=holmes+rahe+stress+scale&o=22837&qsrc=999&l=sem&askid=9916ce56-9147-4f81-9ccd-8f488aa4b406-0-ab_msb.

Personal injury or illness	53
Marriage	50
Fired at work	50
Marital reconciliation with mate	45
Retirement	47
Major change in health of family member	44
Pregnancy	40
Sex difficulties	39
Gain of new family member	39
Major business readjustment	39
Major change in financial state	38
Death of a close friend	37
Changing to a different line of work	37
Death of a close friend	36
Major change in number of adjustments	36
Taking on a mortgage	31
Foreclosure on a mortgage or loan	30
Major change in responsibilities at work	29
In-law troubles	29
Outstanding personal achievement	28
Spouse begin or stop work	26
Beginning or ceasing formal schooling	26
Change in living conditions	25
Change of personal habits	24
Troubles with the boss	23
Major changes in working hours or conditions	20
Changes in residence	20
Changing to a new school	20
Major change in usual type of recreation	19
Major change in church activity	19
Major change in social activities	18
Taking on a loan	17

Major change in sleeping habits	16
Major change in number of family get-togethers	15
Major change in eating habits	15
Vacation	13
Major holidays	12
Minor violation of the law	11
My Total Score:	

Directions: If an event mentioned above has occurred in the past year, or is expected in the near future, copy the number in the score column. If the event has occurred or is expected to occur more than once, multiply this number by the frequency of the event.

Score of 300+: At risk of illness

Score of 150–299: Risk of illness is moderate (reduced by 30% from the above risk)

Score <150: Only have a slight risk of illness.[56]

Believe in Yourself

The idea of being a failure or a success as a caregiver can only be determined by the individual caregiver. Each situation and set of circumstances are different. We each have our own definitions of success and can only do what is right and as our hearts tell us. As caregivers, pastors, and Christian counselors, we need to remind ourselves and our clients that we cannot be guided by guilt, remarks, or opinions from others when we know that under the circumstances we did everything possible that could be done at that time. Caregivers frequently need to be reminded that we all have 20/20 hindsight and can second-guess decisions that were made for years to come. There is still no way of knowing if one's hindsight or second-guessing would have created a different

---

[56] T. H. Holmes and T. H. Rahe, "The Social Adjustment Rating Scale," 11, no. 2 (August 1967).

outcome in most situations. Undue stress and unnecessary guilt feelings are about the only true results that come from second-guessing oneself. Each caregiver goes into this with different experiences, expectations, and life circumstances. "Caregiving is a role with many dimensions and contexts. Understanding the stress and resiliency caregivers experience can be helpful in ministering to their needs,"[57] Northern noted. Galatians 6:2 adds, "Carry each other's heavy loads. If you do, you will give the law of Christ its full meaning." There is a considerable number of opportunities with the graying of America for the Church to help caregivers lessen their burdens.

For many of us, this has been a difficult chapter to read. We thought that we had this caregiving thing figured out, then all this new information was presented. Information that who knew would need to be considered when becoming a caregiver. It is best to look at the new information in the proper context. What type of quality of life would the caregiver, care receiver, and others involved have if the personalities were such polar opposites that there was always tension, yelling, anger, or any number of other behavior concerns? It is better to realize now than after the fact that the best decision is not to be the primary caregiver. There are many horror stories about individuals becoming a caregiver after every indication was present that this was not going to end positively. One is not honoring one's mother or father in this situation. The devil would like to make one feel it is their responsibility and heap piles of guilt upon them. There are many other ways an individual can honor and assist their parents. One would not move their parent into their home if the parent's medical condition required more assistance than they could supply. Having personality differences is similar; we may not be able to visibly see these emotional differences but they are there, and they are out of our skill level of care.

---

[57]   Vicki Moore Northern, "Family Caregiving of the Elderly Parent."

Purposeful Thought and Talk through Questions

Here is an opportunity to go deeper into the chapter. By using the discussion questions below, you have an opportunity through self-talk, counseling, or a small group session to discuss scenarios and to think about different options through engaging in conversation. These questions are not designed to be controversial or divisive. There are no right or wrong answers because each individual and family have different life situations and experiences.

1. Have your thoughts changed any on caregiver duties and their responsibilities? Why, or why not?
2. After reading about burnout and the possible effects, in what ways has it changed your mind about caregivers?
3. In what ways do you think it would be beneficial to discuss possible caregiver scenarios with your family?
4. How do you think Nora's pride might have led her to burnout?
5. Should we volunteer or wait for an individual to ask for our help as a caregiver? Explain your decision. What are some ways that you can help?

CHAPTER 4

WHERE YOU LIVE MAKES A DIFFERENCE

"And even though my illness was a trial to you, you did not treat me with contempt or scorn. Instead, you welcomed me as if I were an angel of God, as if I were Christ Jesus himself"

(GALATIANS 4:14)

Melisa, her sister Michelle, and her brother Roberto were basically the only three family members left. They had a couple of cousins in another state who they had met once, over thirty years ago. Melisa was the "good girl," as her sister Michelle liked to call her; Michelle called herself the bratty baby sister and Roberto the "quiet one." She was the only one who called her siblings by these names that she had given them back in elementary school. They just went along with her since she was the baby of the family.

When Roberto asked his sisters to meet him for lunch, they knew something was amiss because this was something that he never did. Melisa and Michelle sat there sipping on their tea, waiting for Mr. Quiet. He rushed in and apologized for being late, ordered some tea, and got right to it. He was not quiet today. He asked his sisters what they thought about their mom living alone in the house. Both of the sisters did not like it, and even stated that they did not know what to do since they did not like her living at home alone anymore. Everyone was in agreement, and then Roberto asked them what they thought about his idea. Roberto said, "I know none of us want Mom in a nursing home. I was late because I was talking to her doctor and he did not see anything wrong if she moved in with one of us. Since we all are retired or have a spouse at home, what about if we move Mom in with us?"

Both the girls said at the same time, "Who is us?"

Roberto went on to explain that "us" was all of "us." He also explained that they could take turns having their mom live with each of their families for three months. Every three months, their mom would move to the next sibling. This way no one would be watching her all the time and they could make plans around their mom's three-month stay. Roberto went on to explain that their mom only needed companionship and supervision most days, and this would be a good way to maintain her quality of life. He also told them that when and if their mom got too sick, then they could discuss other placement options. He reminded them that their mom got a small check each month and whoever she was staying with could use the money for expenses. Roberto then said, "Take a few days to think about it and talk to your families, and we will meet up again on Friday at Michelle's favorite restaurant at one o'clock." Everyone agreed and proceeded to give their order to the waitress who had just walked up.

If one has not already discovered by now, they will before we finish this chapter: there are a lot of components to consider when taking on the responsibilities of a caregiver. Each family member, and the family, is different and unique in their own way. We all need different components to be applied to our personal caregiving situation. However, there is one theme that remains constant when it comes to being a caregiver: the more you know, the easier it is to help others. It is hard to make decisions that affect one's own loved ones even when they know what the best choice is at the time. The individual's strength weakens, and they waiver when decisions are so close to home. They are not used to making decisions for their parents; it just does not seem right. But it will have to because this is the new way of life.

Individual Preferences

Having to choose or modify a living arrangement is never easy. Of the 21.8 million households headed by older persons, 80 percent were owners and 20 percent were renters in 2001.[58] The "baby boomers" are those born between 1946 and 1964. They started turning sixty-five in 2011, and the number of older people will increase dramatically during the 2014–2030 period. The older population in 2030 is projected to be twice as large as their counterparts in 2000, growing from 35 million to 74 million and representing nearly 21 percent of the total U.S. population. As the older population grows larger, it will also grow more diverse, reflecting the demographic changes in the U.S. population as a whole over the last several decades. By 2060, programs and services for older people will require greater flexibility to meet the needs of a more diverse population.[59]

As a person ages, they generally require more assistance and become more dependent upon outside help and assistance. Everyone has a preference and lifestyle that they would like to maintain. Some individuals prefer to live alone, whereas other individuals thrive on the company and assistance of others. The baby boomers seem to be in denial about their fast-approaching golden years. They deny they are approaching and put forth very little effort to plan for their future, as Robert Blancato explained when he served as executive director for a White House Conference on Aging. He believes that the Baby Boomer suffers from what he calls the "three D" syndrome. They delay, deny, and demand. They have delayed the saving and planning for their senior years. They deny they are aging and demand action when they want something.[60]

---

[58] United States Government, *Older Americans 2004 Key Indicators of Well-Being*.

[59] Ibid.

[60] "Old Age," 2004, accessed February 22, 2005, http://www.realtime.net/wdoud/topics/oldage.html.

External Preferences

What and where are the housing options? It has been reported that there are over forty-five thousand different housing options available for senior citizens. There are over fifteen thousand nursing homes and approximately thirty thousand residential care facilities/homes in the United States.[61] The availability and location are dictated by market demand in most instances. In the larger cities there are more choices and locations to choose from, but that does not always translate into availability or acceptable care. Also, depending on the time of year the vacancies can vary significantly. During the holiday season and summer there are generally more resident room openings. This can be attributed to more family members being available to help take on the role as a caregiver. Some older people living in the community have access to additional services through their place of residence. These services may include meal preparation, laundry, cleaning services, and assistance with medications. These services are designed through the place of residence to help them maintain their independence and avoid transferring to another location where services are directed at those individuals who are less able to care for themselves.

The living arrangements of the older population are important indicators because they are linked to income, health status, and the availability of caregivers. Older Americans who live alone are more prone than other older people who live with their spouses to live in poverty.[62]

Older women were more likely to live alone than older men. In 2015, about 45 percent of the women and 7 percent of the men lived with their spouses. Almost twice as many older women, 36 percent, were as likely to live alone compared to 20 percent of the men. The living arrangements of older people differed by race and Hispanic origin. Older Asian women were more likely to live with relatives other than a spouse. Older

---

[61] United States Government, National Center for Health Statistics, last modified May 3, 2017, accessed September 17, 2017, https://www.cdc.gov/nchs/fastats/nursing-home-care.htm.

[62] United States Government, "Older Americans 2004 Key Indicators of Well-Being."

non-Hispanic white women were 37 percent and black women, 43 percent, were more likely than others to live alone. These statistics show us that here is the opportunity for even the smallest church to be involved in a senior ministry. Since many of these individuals are living alone and lonely, some ideas for helping those old saints are:

1. Card ministry: Sending cards and letters to those who have difficulties getting out of the house
2. Telephone ministry: Calling those individuals who do not get many visits or telephone calls, to check on them and pray with them
3. Visitation: Personal visitation of those who live in the neighborhood, or who were previous members or attendees and also do not receive many visitors
4. Holiday meals: Could be brought to those who do not get out much, or do not have family to visit

These are just a few simple suggestions that could be implemented at about any church. In fact, these projects could be divided up among another church ministries, such as the men's, women's, children's, or missions ministry as a project for the month. Each month another ministry would be the service provider, and continue rotating the duties each month so that a single ministry does not become overwhelmed.

Alternative Housing Arrangements

There are a significant number of alternative living arrangements available for an individual who is unable to safely live at home alone. Each living arrangement is designed to provide a specific level of care and services, depending upon the established admittance criteria. The alternative living market is continually evolving as the adult population ages. As the market expands, there are an increasing number of terms that are used to describe living options. Many of these names are regional and, in some instances, either outdated terminology or new and evolving descriptive terms used to address the changes in society.

Joint Living with Adult Children

This type of living arrangement is when the parent moves into the home of the child/caregiver. This arrangement is also the one that generally has the least amount of success because the decision is based on emotion, not fact. Before this type of living arrangement is even considered, all possible scenarios should be evaluated. Some possible areas of concern should be:

1. What do the other family members in the home think of this type of arrangement?
2. Is the dwelling large enough, and what personal possessions will the parent want to bring?
3. Is the home safe and free of obstacles?
4. Can the parent be left home alone, or do they need constant supervision?
5. Does the potential caregiver's lifestyle allow for them to be at home more?
6. Can the potential caregiver release their privacy?
7. Do the personalities of the potential caregiver and care receiver mesh or conflict with each other and other members in the house?

As has been demonstrated in previous sections, there are multiple options to every caregiver decision that they might make. Besides all the options available, the industry terminology can be overwhelming. Below are some of the most frequent types of senior housing and a definition of each one.

- Staying home by scaling down: This is when a relatively healthy and independent senior citizen moves into a smaller residence because they can no longer care for a larger residence.

- Elder Cottage Housing Opportunity (ECHO) or Tiny House: This is the placing of a pre-build, self-contained cottage, also known as "granny flats," in the back or side yard of a single-family house. This type of arrangement allows for the parents to live next to their children while both households are able to retain most of their privacy. These housing units include barrier-free features and can be designed to fit the current building structure design, style, and color. Some units can be rented, installed, and removed when no longer needed. The Elder Cottage Housing Opportunity concept is credited with originating in Australia.
- Home sharing: The idea of home sharing is when someone other than a child moves into the home or apartment. The arrangements and caregiving duties depend on what the individuals have agreed upon. In some instances, the individual moving in agrees to help with a particular list of tasks and caregiving tasks in exchange for free rent, partial rent, or paycheck and rent for caregiver services rendered.
- Accessory apartment: In this variation on home sharing, your parent's home is remodeled to include a self-contained apartment with a separate entrance. The apartment can be rented out to gain income or services can be rendered in exchange for free or reduced rent.
- Adult foster care: This type of housing is generally for those who are "frail" but in reasonably good health. Adult foster homes provide lodging, meals, supervision, and no medical personal care. Most homes are privately owned and have one to twenty residents, depending upon the size of the home and state regulations.
- Congregate housing: This type of housing includes retirement hotels and retirement apartments. The services vary, depending on price, location, and state. Generally one or more meals are

offered daily, while housekeeping, recreation, transportation, and security are offered on a limited basis.

- Retirement communities: Included in this type of housing are apartments, mobile homes, townhomes, condominiums, and cooperatives developed especially for senior citizens who are capable of living alone relatively safely.

- Assisted-living facilities: This is a fairly new type of housing and is also known as personal-care homes, residential-care facilities, and sheltered-care and adult-care homes. These are places for older adults who need some assistance with daily living activities but do not require skilled nursing care.

- Continuing Care Retirement Communities (CCRC): They offer varying levels of care. They start with the resident not requiring assistance and progress in levels, up to providing some assistance with daily living activities. The independent level is where the individual can live alone safely. Whenever there is a level decline in independence, the resident is moved to a residential area where more care is required.

- Nursing homes: This is a facility where twenty-four-hour health care and services are provided. This type of facility has the worst stigma and psychological attachments to the old folk's home, retirement home, and skilled nursing facility due to the pure nature of their business: caring for the elderly who are sick, disabled, and nearing the end of their life expectancy. The poor services and care of a small percentage of nursing homes have caused a negative view of this type living facility.

There are options available to assist the caregiver when they are looking to find an alternative care living arrangement, but what are they? Where are they? Can they really help? It is not only very stressful having to make the decision that a family member cannot live at home alone safely, but having to find alternate living arrangements can be even more stressful. In most instances, the family will be forced to look for and decide on an alternate housing arrangement because the senior family member has gotten ill or had an accident, and the physician is recommending that the parent move to some type of care facility where there is a twenty-four-hour care available. Most individuals do not know where to look, what to look for, or what questions to ask the care facility.

This is where the Christian counselor can be a tremendous support and resource.

Knowing where to look for a care facility and what questions to ask can relieve a family of a tremendous burden. The caregiver can locate information through various local or national organizations, churches, hospitals, libraries, publications, websites, and brochures. The following guides and brochures are designed to be used as a resource. The care facility guides are designed to try to get answers to some of the frequently asked questions during a visit. The second form is designed to make telephone inquiries before the visit so that a list of possible choices can be narrowed down, especially when time is limited. It is very beneficial when the telephone-screening form is used if someone else can assist so that information can be compared and a decision can be made as to which care facilities warrant a visit. The resource helps fact sheet in the appendix is a compilation of information that a caregiver, a Christian counselor, or a pastor might find beneficial on health-care organizations, websites, resource books, and where to locate information about housing options. Please refer to Appendix B: Exhibit 1 for Senior Housing Guide Checklist; please refer to Appendix B: Exhibit 2 for Care Facility Profile.

Health-Care Provider Availability

As one comes closer to making the decision that they will become the primary caregiver, the next step is to determine the best place for the care receiver to live. As a caregiver, it is important to know what is required in this step and what will be involved in its completion. First, is the care receiver open to changing physicians, specialists, hospitals, or churches if the distance is too great to continue to use the health-care providers that they are currently using? Services will continue to be available, but will they change as health care changes? More and more baby boomers are planning on staying home during their golden years as long as possible. Some seniors are moving into housing communities that offer health and wellness programs. The shortage of medical personnel is predicted to grow as the number of baby boomers increases. This could have a negative impact on the type of medical services offered in an area, including less direct care by physicians, higher medical cost, increased home health cost, over-the-counter purchases, and natural remedies.

Many times the choice that an individual will make concerning senior housing options has to be made immediately; even with both limited resources and limited knowledge concerning available choices, a decision must be made. As we progress into the twenty-first century there will be few adult children and family members whose lives will not be touched directly or indirectly by an aging loved one who needs some measure of care. According to the U.S. Census Bureau, the number of centenarians will be over fifty-three thousand in 2010, and by 2060, the number could reach a total of six hundred thousand centenarians, one-hundred-year-old men and women.[63] The older population sixty-five years and older numbered 47.8 million in 2015. The projected number of Americans aged sixty-five years and older in 2060 will comprise nearly 25 percent of the U.S. residents and 19.7 million will be over eighty-five years old. In 2016, 57.8 percent of the population sixty-five years and older were married, and 25 percent of those sixty-five years and older were widowed.[64] Our society is aging and living longer thanks to the fields of nutrition, science, and medicine; our life expectancy has reached a new high.

The statistics above demonstrate how America is graying. The Church now has the opportunity to step up to the plate and help those who can

---

[63] United States Government, "Older Americans 2004 Key Indicators of Well-Being," August 2016, accessed September 20, 2016, https://agingstats.gov/docs/LatestReport/Older-Americans-2016-Key-Indicators-of-WellBeing.pdf.

[64] "Marital Status and Living Arrangements," accessed November 17, 2017, http://www.census.gov/hhes/families/data/cps2016.

use a little help and companionship. We are instructed in James to look after widows and orphans in distress. Do we just ignore our elders? Are they not our Judea and Samaria? Whether one belongs to a large church or a small one, there are a number of things that can be done to help the elderly that can cost little to nothing.

First Things First

When evaluating the potential living arrangements, there are several tasks that will need to be completed if they have not already been done. One of those tasks is an emergency call contact list. This is a very valuable and time-saving document to have in an emergency. No matter where the care receiver moves to, this form is a must. In the event of an emergency, when one is asked what the care receiver's specialist's name is, which pharmacy they use, or their phone number, the individual prepared with this emergency call contact list will have the information already. This form should be on the caregiver's phone, in their purse or wallet, and posted on the refrigerator. Even if there are no current health issues, it is prudent to be prepared for an accident. In the event of a sudden illness or accident, the names and numbers of the physicians who are familiar with the parent are at hand. There is no rushing to their house looking for information that may or may not even be current. The individual has what is needed in the event of an emergency and can concentrate on traveling to the health-care facility where their loved one is receiving medical care. Please refer to Appendix B: Exhibit 3 for Emergency Call Contact List.

A family caregiver will know most of the information that will be required to complete an emergency call. This should be compiled in advance and posted or made available for possible future use. This contact list will also allow others to help and make telephone calls while the primary caregiver tends to another task if needed.

What are some of the duties that the caregiver needs to immediately undertake since they have decided to take on the role of primary caregiver? Home safety is very important, and it is prudent to be safety conscious. As one ages, they do not heal, ambulate, or react as quickly as they did when they were younger. Depending on why someone is requiring caregiver assistance, this person may have deficits in a couple of areas. They may have arthritis so they do not move as quickly, or early onset of dementia or Alzheimer's, which has caused them to be more forgetful or confused than in their younger days.

There is an enormous physical, psychological, and economic toll when an older person becomes injured. Falls among older people can be caused by hazards involving both internal and external factors. Older women experience more falls than older men, and these women are more likely to live alone. The frequency and severity of accidents in the home of older people emphasize the need for modifications to the home to compensate for the declining physical functions of the individual. The most common accident sites in the home are the bathroom, kitchen, bedroom, and stairs; the most hazardous room in the house is the bedroom. This is where falls, fires, poisoning, and suffocation may occur.[65] There will be additional information in more detail on home modifications and assistive technology in an upcoming chapter.

Medical Care Options

Predicting what type of treatments patients will want at the end of life is complicated by:

- the individual's age;
- the nature of the illness;
- the ability of medical science and pharmacology to sustain life;
- the emotions of the family, patient requests, and medical diagnosis outcomes;[66]

---

[65] Margaret A. Christianson, *Aging in the Designed Environment* (Binghamton, NY: Haworth Press, 1990), 55.

[66] Ellen D. Taira, *Aging in Place: Designing, Adapting, and Enhancing the Home Environment* (Binghamton, New York: Haworth Press, 2002), 77.

- the fact that less than 50 percent of the severely or terminally ill had an advance directive;
- the fact that over 70 percent of physicians whose patients had advance directives were not aware that it existed; and
- surrogates named in the advance directives were often not present to make decisions or were too emotionally overwrought to offer guidance.

Preparing for illness or death is not the most popular topic of discussion during dinner. The subject itself of an advance directive, wills, or funeral arrangements does not motivate a smile. But as a person feels that natural response of resistance to not have a conversation, they could instead view this as a wonderful opportunity to learn more about this important topic. The topics are important and some areas will be more applicable today and others in the probable near future. By having discussed the information with those involved and having the information readily available, one can make it easier for one's spouse or family in the event of illness or death. They know the decisions have been made, they know the caregiver's desires, and they have been instructed on what the care receiver would like done. It is not easy, but they will know the will of the care receiver. Those involved might not agree with the care receiver's decision, but it is their decision and one that should be honored no matter how difficult that might be.

Advance Planning a Practical Part of Aging

Advance planning is a way to protect the whole family and let everyone know what has been decided so that there is no questioning, second-guessing, or fighting. Individuals with chronic diseases go through periods of slowly declining health marked by severe episodes that require hospitalization. This sequence can be repeated a number of times as the patient's health continues to decline, and they finally expire. A legal document known as a medical directive or an advance directive can assist in eliminating a significant amount of confusion, guilt, and arguing among family members. These documents declare the care receiver's wishes regarding life support or other medical treatment in certain circumstances, usually when death is imminent.

Life is sacred, and each individual should have his wishes documented well in advance concerning end-of-life decisions. On their website, the National Hospice and Palliative Care Organization has advance directives and living will forms for most states. There are many variations of these forms on other websites, and an attorney could also compile the information for this type of document. For educational purposes, the appendices include a sample of one type of living will, durable power of attorney, and instructions applicable in the state of Georgia.[67] Whether a caregiver, a Christian counselor, a pastor, or a care receiver, one should investigate completing advance directives and obtain the proper documentation, completed and filed with the appropriate agencies. If there are any questions concerning the documents or their proper meaning, each counselee should discuss their questions with a medical professional and an attorney so there are no mixed messages or assumptions made by those concerned.

Summary of Latter Life Activity

How active is the parent? Filling time with events is not the objective. The objective is to provide enjoyable and familiar activities. Being entertained by others does not fulfill one's fundamental needs. Senior adults need activities that allow them to identify themselves as persons of worth and ability who are significantly related to others. There is nothing improper with modifying activities as needed. The activities of older adults usually demonstrate the following characteristics:

- Most older individuals do not sit around with nothing to do. They have developed routines and activities over the years that usually fill their day and evening.

---

[67] "Advance Directives," accessed May 5, 2005, http://www.caringinfo.org/i4a/pages/index.cfm?pageid=1&activateFull=false.

- The individuals who are the most satisfied with their lives usually engage in regular activities outside the home that present challenges and nurture relationships with friends and family.
- The activities do not usually occur in age-segregated settings.
- The activities that are the most significant are usually those that were satisfying in earlier years. The active older adult does select, replace, and even start new activities. They enjoy and value these activities because they have established identities, competencies, self-images, values, and relationships.
- The activities that are most likely to attract older adults are built upon familiarity, interaction, established abilities and identities, and histories of satisfaction. What generally makes activity programs attractive is their quality rather than any age designation.
- Activity programs that require older adults to redefine themselves as old, inferior, or incompetent are probably not going to be well attended.

Both personal and social histories are important in the development of activity interest and abilities.[68] The care receiver in some instances will not mention wanting to be involved in outside activities. They will not say that they would not mind going to the senior center, church group, or club because they think they are bothering others. Some older adults believe they need to stay at the house with the caregiver since they are now living with them.

An individual might have played eighteen holes of golf weekly but recently stopped since the arthritis in the knees has worsened, and they have not played golf in almost two years. Some alternatives could be developed, such as a putting green in the yard or taking the individual to the golf course to practice hitting golf balls on the driving range.

---

[68] Mathy Menzey, *The Encyclopedia of Elder Care* (Amherst, NY: Prometheus Books, 2004), 9.

Another example of a modified activity might be using assistive technology for someone who has declining vision. If the individual enjoyed reading in the past and has difficulties seeing now, some modifications might be large-print books, books on tape, Closed Captioning on Television (CC), magnifier, or talking devices. Doing so will allow them to enjoy some of the activities they took part in before their declining health.

It is imperative that the caregiver work judiciously in providing as stress free an environment as possible. The benefits are innumerable when one is in the right environment; depression is decreased or eliminated, and there is improvement in health, attitude, motivation, and outlook, to name just a few of the outcomes. Having said this, just a few modifications can make for a better relationship and quality of life for all involved.

To Exercise or Not to Exercise

Why does exercise help us live longer? The first of two of the primary reasons is that exercise helps the body resist disease, triggered by priming the immune system's cells that protect against disease. Second, exercise improves blood circulation, keeping the body and brain in good condition and helping one to resist primary aging.[69] An advocate for staying active in the later years, Dr. Josef P. Hirachovee said, "Exercise is the closest thing to an anti-aging pill now available. It acts like a miracle and it's free for the doing."[70] Research has shown us that physical activity is beneficial for the health of people of all ages, including those sixty-five years and over. Physical activity can reduce the risk of certain chronic diseases, may relieve symptoms of depression, helps to maintain independent living, and enhances overall quality of life. Scientific research has shown

---

[69] Leonard Biegel, *Physical Fitness and the Older Person: A Guide to Exercise for Health Care Professionals* (Rockville, MD: Aspens Systems Corporation, 1984), 30.

[70] Joe P. Hiavochee, *Keeping Young and Living Longer* (Los Angeles, CA: Sherbourne Press, 1972), 129.

that even among the frail and very old adults, mobility and functioning can be improved through physical activity.

The percentage of people sixty-five years and older engaging in regular leisure time physical activity was 21 percent in 2001–2002. Men over sixty-five were more likely than women in the same age group to report being involved in some type of regular leisure physical activity. There are several other types of physical activities that contribute to overall health and fitness. Strength training has been recommended as part of a comprehensive physical activity program among older adults and may help to improve balance and decrease risk of falls. What can be done to help prevent or delay the onset of chronic diseases such as coronary heart disease, certain types of cancer, stroke, and Type 2 diabetes? A healthy diet can reduce some major risk factors for chronic diseases, such as obesity, high blood pressure, and high blood cholesterol.

Senior centers began in the United States in the early 1940s. Today there are between 10,000 and 12,000 centers in the United States. A majority of the elderly know where these centers are located in their community. A vast majority of the senior centers are multipurpose and offer a wide range of health, social, recreational, and educational services. The Older Americans Act (OAA) has focused on these types of centers to serve as community focal points for comprehensive service coordination and delivery at the local level. Senior centers provide services for seniors as well as important information and referrals through connections with a variety of organizations, local, state, and government programs. These centers are often used by other agencies as delivery centers for programs such as congregate meals and health education.[71]

The larger senior centers usually have paid staff and also rely on volunteers to assist. Research has suggested that the users of these senior centers generally have higher levels of health, social interaction, and life satisfaction as well as lower levels of income than nonusers. Many of the senior centers in larger cities, suburbs, and rural areas are facing

---

[71] Menzey, *The Encyclopedia of Elder Care*, 586.

challenges and opportunities associated with the increasing numbers of seniors from diverse ethnic backgrounds.[72]

According to Bucher, many seniors and their families are confused because of the lack of easy access to information, misunderstanding of the aging and disease process, and lack of relevant information available to the general public.[73] This in turn causes additional turmoil and stress upon the individual, family, and caregiver. Many individuals continue to struggle alone with their problems, not knowing which way to turn until they are forced to make a decision with little or no information due to an emergency situation. Finding out about available services, as well as knowing how to qualify and use them, is very important.

Purposeful Thought and Talk through Questions

Here is an opportunity to go deeper into the chapter. By using these questions, one can discuss scenarios and think about different options through self-talk, counseling, or a small group session. These questions are not designed to be controversial or divisive. There are no right or wrong answers because each individual and family have different life situations and experiences.

1. Why is important to know if the care receiver is willing to move from their current home or out of the area? What are the options available if they are resistant to moving?
2. What type of housing option would the caregiver like when it is eventually time for them to move? Have they made their family aware of their wishes?
3. Has the caregiver discussed advance directives with their parents? Have they discussed advance directives with their children? Why, or why not?

---

[72] Ibid.

[73] Arianne Stoppelenburg, "The Effects of Advance Care Planning on End of Life Care," September 1, 2014, accessed January 2, 2018, https://eapcnet.wordpress.com/2014/09/01/the-effects-of-advance-care-planning

4. Does the Church have a responsibility to visit and assist the local elderly? Why, or why not? Should the Church only visit church members? Why, or why not?
5. What happens at one's church after an elderly church member is not able to drive or get around?

CHAPTER 5

SOLUTIONS FOR PROBLEMS
YOU DID NOT KNOW
WERE THERE

"Love is patient, love is kind. It does not envy, it does not boast, it is not proud. It does not dishonor others, it is not self-seeking, it is not easily angered, it keeps no record of wrongs. Love does not delight in evil but rejoices with the truth. It always protects, always trusts, always hopes, always perseveres"

(1 CORINTHIANS 13:4 –7)

Marco was starting to get worried about his father, who had a stroke about a year ago. His mom was taking care of him, and they had set up respite care for his mother, and home health care every day for a couple of hours in the morning and again in the evening. Right now, it seemed that they had all of the help they needed. Mom was able to get a rest when the home-health agency came or when one of the children came over at least once a week to give her a break. They had help every day for bathing, as well as at mealtimes for breakfast and dinner to feed Dad. There was help to get Dad out of bed in the morning and into bed in the evening. The home-health agency also helped with bathing three days a week. In addition there was help to get him in and out of the wheelchair and put him to bed in the afternoon for a nap.

The family had heard horror stories about not having enough, so they made sure as a family that there would always be enough help for Dad so that Mom didn't end up sick also. Marco was worried about his dad; even though things seemed to be going well, he just didn't look right. Marco had a friend from church who was an occupational therapist at a local hospital. He was not sure what his friend did, but he decided to call him anyway and ask him what he thought. They set up a time to meet for coffee in a few days, and Marco wrote down his concerns so that he didn't forget any. When they met up for coffee, his friend Eli explained what he did as an occupational therapist at the rehab center. As he was talking about his profession, lights and bells started to go off in Marco's head. He wondered why he had waited so long to call Eli.

As a result of their meeting, Eli said he "would be glad to come out the next day and make some suggestions that might help." Eli came out and was there about two hours, looking the house over, speaking to both Mom and Dad, and reviewing the home-health schedule. Eli and Marco made plans to meet up again in a few days. Marco was anxious for the meeting so he could find out what Eli thought. When they met again, Eli stated that he thought the family had done a good job with getting help and taking care of their father. He said that he had a couple of suggestions, but they would need to be followed consistently if they were going to be successful.

First, Eli thought they should make an appointment to take their father to his physician to determine if he was suffering from depression. Eli reminded the family that in their hurry to take care of their dad physically, they might have forgotten about him mentally. Marco went on to explain that until the day that his father had the stroke he was up and about, a very independent person. Now, after having the stroke, he needed help for almost everything, especially since he had limited use of his left arm and shoulder. Eli went on, saying that he was going to recommend some assistive devices that would help their father be more independent, but because of his condition, he would probably always need support other than these devices. Eli explained that these assistive technology devices should help and give their father some feelings of independence and self-worth. The device would help increase his independence by 10 to 25 percent. He went on to explain that it might not sound like much, but it was if one was going from 100 percent assistance.

Eli suggested starting with a curved spoon, since their dad had the most difficulties feeding himself. Because of the limited use of their father's left arm and shoulder, Eli also suggested a sock-aid to assist with putting on socks and a button hook, something that was used to button buttons. When Eli explained to their dad what they were doing, his face lit up with excitement. He could not wait to learn how to use the first round of assistive devices. Dad was the most pleased with the spoon. Even though he was able to only feed himself about 25 percent of the meal, he was elated. No more feeling like a child getting fed; now he felt like he was contributing to his own life and not just having someone do everything for him.

Good Health, Bad Health, Does It Matter?

The Individual's Health Condition

The health of the individual is as significant as their financial resources when the parent and their family are determining what decisions to make. In many instances, the health of the individual determines the housing arrangement and whether an assisted living center, home care, personal-care home, or a nursing home is the best option. All of these housing selections offer different levels of care, financial costs, and cater to the varying likes and dislikes an individual may have. As we age and changes occur in our vision, cognition, mobility, hearing, and manual dexterity, home adaptations can be a necessity.

Chronic diseases are long-term illnesses that are rarely cured, and generally the individual's health deteriorates over time. Some of the most common and most costly chronic diseases include heart disease, stroke, cancer, and diabetes. Chronic health conditions affect the quality of life negatively, contributing to declines in functioning and many times the inability to remain in the home. In many instances, behavioral interventions could have prevented or modified the health outcomes of many of the chronic illnesses within our society. The six leading chronic diseases among people sixty-five years of age and older are:

1. Influenza and pneumonia
2. Chronic lower respiratory diseases
3. Stroke
4. Alzheimer's disease
5. Cancer
6. Diabetes

Heart disease and cancer were the top two leading causes of death in 2014 among all people age sixty-five years and over. The occurrence of chronic conditions differs by sex. Statistics show that women report higher levels of hypertension, asthma, chronic bronchitis, and arthritic symptoms. Men reported higher incidences of heart disease, cancer, diabetes, and emphysema.[74]

Self-Assessed Health Status

The respondent-assessed health ratings of good, very good, and excellent correlate with lower risk of mortality. The purpose of asking people to rate their health using one of the categories provides a common indicator of health easily measured in surveys. It represents the physical, emotional, and social aspect of health and well-being. Of older persons age sixty-five years and older, 78 percent assessed their health as good, very good, or excellent during the 2012–2014 period. The older that individual was, the lower he rated his health, with 68 percent of those eighty-five years and

---

[74] Federal Interagency Forum on Aging-Related Statistics, "2016 Older Americans Key Indicators of Well-Being," August 2016, accessed September 12, 2017, http://agingstats.gov/.

over rating their health as better or good. These statistics are helpful in letting one know that their perception of their health is not always its true picture. There are not very many people who will admit that their health is declining and that they are experiencing age-related difficulties. When one admits they are having aging difficulties, then they have to start facing the fact that their life expectancy is real and that they will not live forever.

Another hidden point that the statistics reveal is that one should not take their parents' words as honest and accurate that they are not having any difficulties. Growing old is difficult in the American society. Our culture does not prepare us for old age and all that it entails. Growing old is not easy in our society. The way in which we age can be dependent upon the way in which one believes that society is viewing their elderly.[75] Even the psalmist was concerned about being cast away in his old age, saying, "Do not cast me away when I am old: do not forsake me when my strength is gone" (Psalm 71:9). Through positive conversation and reassurance with one's parents, they can demonstrate to them that aging is a natural process and that they are concerned about their safety. One of the best ways to help a parent is to visit one's parent regularly or have a trusted family member or friend who knows the care receiver to visit regularly and take note if there are any changes. This visitor can check on the parent by answering the following questions during the visit:

1. Is the care receiver declining in his previous housekeeping duties?
2. Is the care receiver able to get around the house without tripping, stumbling, or falling?
3. How is the care receiver's balance? Do they need help getting up from sitting on the sofa or a chair?
4. Is the care receiver leaving pans on the stove or losing items in the house?

---

[75] Richard Gentzler, *Aging and Ministry in the 21st Century* (Nashville, TN: Discipleship Resources, 2008), 19.

These are a few of the everyday life skills that will indicate if it is time to make a change in the current arrangement. In some instances, the care receiver might not be having any trouble until they are stricken with an illness or one of the chronic diseases, and will then require caregiving assistance and housing arrangement changes.

Can I Still Live at Home?

There are several conditions that can affect the elderly and limit their ability to live at home independently. Some of the conditions that can limit one's ability to live at home will be detailed briefly in the following sections.

Arthritis

Arthritis affects about one in every six Americans. The two most common forms of arthritis are osteoarthritis and rheumatoid arthritis. Arthritis is a term that means joint inflammation and is a leading cause of disability in the United States. Typically arthritis makes the joints painful, stiff, and swollen, and this can turn the simplest of everyday tasks into a painful ordeal that requires assistance to complete.[76]

Memory Impairment

Memory skills are important to general cognitive functioning, and declining scores on memory tests are one of several indicators that there is a cognitive loss of functioning. Low cognitive functioning such as memory impairment is a major health and safety risk factor to consider when con-templating which type of caregiving situation to implement. Depending on the severity of the memory impairment, in-home care is feasible at times, while in other circumstances moving the individual and entering a nursing

---

[76] Federal Interagency Forum on Aging-Related Statistics, "Older Americans 2004: Key Indicators of Well-Being," November 1, 2004, accessed May 1, 2017, https://agingstats. gov/docs/PastReports/2004/OA2004.pdf.

home are the best option. Each set of choices and family circumstances are different; there is no one answer or formula that works for everyone.

Older men are more likely to experience memory impairment of moderate to severe intensity than are older women; the percentage of men age sixty-five years and over who experienced moderate to severe memory impairment was slightly higher than that of women.[77] Approximately one-third of both men and women experienced moderate or severe memory impairment. Moderate or severe memory impairment is six times as high for people age eighty-five years and over than those individuals sixty-five to sixty-nine years of age.[78] Alzheimer's is not the only disease that causes memory impairments or a decline in cognitive functioning, but it is the one that is the most recognized. Alzheimer's disease is not a normal part of aging. This disease affects the individual's brain nerve cells that impair memory, thinking, and ultimately leads to death. There are an estimated 4.5 million individuals who have Alzheimer's disease. The number of Americans with this disease will continue to grow, and by the year 2050, the number of individuals with Alzheimer's is estimated to be between 11.3 million and 16 million. Age is the greatest risk factor; risk increases as an individual ages. One in ten people over sixty-five and nearly half of those over eighty-five years old are affected. A person with Alzheimer's disease will live an average of eight years and as many as twenty years from initial onset.[79]

Diabetes

The cause of diabetes is still unknown. This is a disease in which the body does not produce or properly use insulin. Insulin is a hormone in the body that is needed for daily living, particularly to convert sugar,

---

[77] Federal Interagency Forum on Aging-Related Statistics, *2016 Older Americans Key Indicators of Well-Being*.

[78] Ibid.

[79] Federal Interagency Forum on Aging-Related Statistics, "Older Americans 2004: Key Indicators of Well-Being," November 1, 2004, accessed May 1, 2017, https://agingstats. gov/docs/PastReports/2004/OA2004.pdf.

starches, and other foods into energy. In the United States, there are 18.2 million people who have diabetes and another 5.2 million people who are unaware they have the disease. Some of the conditions that can be caused by diabetes are impaired vision, stroke, slow healing or nonhealing wounds, body weight issues, and neuropathy.[80]

Sensory Impairments

The quality of life is limited for the elderly as their hearing, vision, and oral manipulation decreases. As the aging population increases over the next thirty years, the number of visual, hearing, and oral impairments should increase. These individuals have more difficulties performing activities of daily living and communicating with others. Older individuals are disproportionately affected by these losses when compared to other age groups. Vision and hearing impairments, as well as oral health problems, are often thought of as natural signs of aging. Early detection and treatment can prevent or postpone some of the debilitating physical, social, and emotional effects these impairments can have on the lives of older individuals. Of individuals sixty-five years old and older in 2014, 8 percent of men and 4 percent of women reported having hearing difficulties. The percentage of those who reported hearing difficulties was higher as the respondent's age increased. Generally, under Medicare insurance, glasses, hearing aids, and regular dental care are not covered services. These services will normally have to be paid for out of pocket, or possibly through another insurance provider.

This Is What I See

The five senses—smell, taste, touch, seeing, and hearing—are important to each of us. As one ages, the senses become less responsive and decline in function to some degree in most individuals. As this paper has

---

[80] Federal Interagency Forum on Aging-Related Statistics, "Older Americans 2004: Key Indicators of Well-Being," November 1, 2004, accessed May 1, 2017, https://agingstats. gov/docs/PastReports/2004/OA2004.pdf.

discussed, all people age at a different rate, and it is the same with our senses; they decline and respond differently for each individual as they get older. It can be devastating to an individual as their senses decline when they have been used to using their vision to see objects in a familiar manner and magnification. Visual impairments affect about 18 percent of the older population; 16 percent of the women and 19 percent of the men are affected by some type of visual impairment. Of those eighty-five years old and over, 33 percent reported having vision impairment. Among those sixty-five years and over who reported vision difficulties, 16 percent reported having had glaucoma, 16 percent reported having macular degeneration, and 44 percent reported having cataracts in the past twelve months.[81] Although one may know the name of the vision impairment their parent has, it can still be difficult to understand and imagine what it is the parent sees with their visual impairment. To aid in a better understanding of the more common age-related vision impairments, the following pages include pictures with descriptions. The photographs will allow the reader to get a visual image of what is viewed by people with specific kinds of vision impairment.

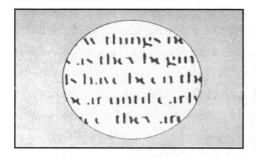 

Figure 1.0: Blurry vision; for example, cataract[82]

---

[81] Federal Interagency Forum on Aging-Related Statistics, "Older Americans 2004: Key Indicators of Well-Being," November 1, 2004, accessed May 1, 2017, https://agingstats.gov/docs/PastReports/2004/OA2004.pdf.

[82] Figures from the National Eye Institute, https://nei.nih.gov/photo.

The most common age-related eye condition is the cataract. It is a clouding of the normally clear and transparent lens of the eye that reduces passages of light. There is increased sensitivity to glare, and everything looks hazy. Cataract surgery is usually recommended when the individual's vision affects their ability to perform everyday tasks. Cataract surgery with a lens implant can restore one's vision to its former clarity.[83]

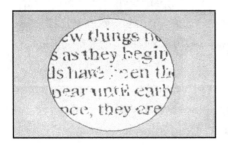 

Figure 1.2: Central loss of vision; for example, macular degeneration[84]

The leading cause of vision loss among older adults is macular degeneration. It is degenerative and causes blurred and distorted central vision. The most common form among older adults is the "dry" form. There are approximately 15 million individuals in the United States who have age-related macular degeneration, and about 16,000 new cases of macular degeneration are diagnosed each year. Scarring occurs in the macular area, the center of the retina, and this creates difficulty in reading, writing, sewing, recognizing faces, and just about anything that requires detailed visual work. Currently there is no cure, but vision rehabilitation can be effective for learning new vision strategies and coping skills. Vision rehabilitation involves restorative services, including low vision assessment, optical aid prescription, training in orientation and mobility, and training in activities of daily living.[85]

---

[83] Ellen D. Taira and Jodi Carlson, *Aging in Place: Designing, Adapting, and Enhancing the Home Environment* (Binghamton, NY: Haworth Press, 2002), 62.

[84] Figures from the National Eye Institute, https://nei.nih.gov/photo.

[85] Ellen D. Taira and Jodi Carlson, *Aging in Place: Designing, Adapting, and Enhancing the Home Environment*, 63.

Figure 1.3: Peripheral loss of vision; for example, glaucoma[86]

Some have called glaucoma the "sneak thief of sight" because it affects the peripheral vision gradually and can be quite advanced before a problem is detected. Open-angle glaucoma affects about 2.5 percent of the population over forty years old and increases with age. The condition is treatable, and an annual glaucoma test performed by a vision specialist is recommended. Early diagnosis and treatment are very important in preventing additional vision loss. The central vision remains intact, so reading is not usually a concern, but orientation and mobility training are crucial.[87]

Figure 1.4: Blind spots/distorted vision; for example, diabetic retinopathy[88]

Diabetic retinopathy is a result of a complication of diabetes. Retinopathy cannot be prevented, but better control and management of diabetes can delay the onset. An individual's vision may fluctuate daily

---

[86] Figures from the National Eye Institute, https://nei.nih.gov/photo.

[87] Ellen D. Taira and Jodi Carlson, *Aging in Place: Designing, Adapting, and Enhancing the Home Environment*, 64.

[88] Figures from the National Eye Institute, https://nei.nih.gov/photo.

from nearly normal to distorted. Damaged blood vessels may leak fluid or blood in the eye, which causes retinal scars that distort the vision and create blind spots. Controlling diabetes is imperative to minimizing its effects on vision.[89]

Oral health is another area in which one may have sensory impairment. The prevalence of edentulism, having no natural teeth, was higher amongst people age eighty-five years and over at 38 percent than for people sixty-five to seventy-four years at 24 percent. Socioeconomic differences appeared to make a difference, with 46 percent of older people with family income below the poverty line reporting no natural teeth compared with 27 percent of people above the poverty threshold.[90] So that one's parent can eat nutritious foods, it might be important that they have regular dental visits.

Rehabilitation Services

The disability rate is disproportionately high among the elderly. In many instances with appropriate rehabilitation services, there can be a restoration of function after an illness or injury has occurred through the use of a variety of interventions directed at the disablement. Rehabilitation intervention services address the patient's ability to interact with the environment through restoration of full independence, modified independence, or assisted functioning. The pathology of some diseases and illnesses may affect the benefit gained from specific rehabilitation interventions or alter the way the interventions are presented. Interventions in rehabilitation services can include, but are not limited to:

1. exercise prescriptions directed by a physician or rehabilitation specialist;

---

[89] Ellen D. Taira and Jodi Carlson, *Aging in Place: Designing, Adapting, and Enhancing the Home Environment*, 65.

[90] Federal Interagency Forum on Aging-Related Statistics, "Older Americans 2004: Key Indicators of Well-Being," November 1, 2004, accessed May 1, 2017, https://agingstats. gov/docs/PastReports/2004/OA2004.pdf.

2. adaptive techniques that include modifications in the way an activity is performed;
3. assistive technology devices that include telephone amplifiers, weighted eating utensils, reachers, canes, walkers, and wheelchairs;
4. physical modalities that include heat, cold, and ultrasound;
5. orthotic devices such as braces, splints, and foot orthotics; and
6. a prosthesis or false limbs.

Regular exercise can help prevent disability and even reduce the extent of disability and counteract the adverse effects of immobility whether due to systematic illness or trauma.[91] Despite physical limitations, adaptive techniques involving the modification of a task are presented so that the patients can retain as much self-independence as possible. By being proficient with adaptive techniques, this allows the patient to be able to interact with his environment in a more positive manner. Some adaptive techniques include learning to dress independently using one arm after having a stroke. The effects from a stroke might be the limited use of one hand, or upper extremity can require one to have to learn new dressing techniques and how to hold items properly so as not to stress the arm and hand joints. There are numerous adaptive techniques, and the use of them depends on the illness and the skill level of the patient.

There are rehabilitation specialists who can assist the physician when the individual is receiving rehabilitation or therapy services. Some of the professionals involved in rehabilitation care are occupational therapists, physical therapists, speech-language therapists, and nursing staff. The services they provide are done in a variety of settings, including hospitals, sub-acute, outpatient, home care, and nursing homes. The treatment services that are provided by rehabilitation therapists follow a treatment plan with measurable functional goals. Rehabilitation education goals are important and could include shaping realistic goals in conjunction with the patient's

---

[91] Mathy Mezey, *The Encyclopedia of Elder Care* (Amherst, NY: Prometheus Books, 2004), 560.

therapy goals and condition, educating patients about their potential for recovery, teaching self-care, and advising patients and caregivers. When physical and cognitive function has been restored to an optimal or maximal level for the patient, a discharge plan is discussed and implemented.[92]

Referral to a rehabilitation specialist can be a significant benefit when assistance is needed to eliminate, minimize, or modify the contextual factors that in many instances magnify or create disabilities. Individuals who are medically unstable may not be candidates for rehabilitation services at that time but may be in the future. This is determined by having the primary care provider reassess the patient regularly so that a proper determination for referring the patient for rehabilitation intervention services can be made. When the prognosis for recovery is encouraging, the negative effects of immobility are easier to prevent than remediate.

What Is the Prognosis?

A thorough discussion with the elderly individual's physician should be arranged before definitive choices are made and significant modifications are applied to a residence. The physician can shed some light on to the aging individual's health condition and what appropriate medical interventions may need to be taken. If an individual is unsure about a home modification and safety assessment, most hospitals or rehabilitation centers employ an occupational or physical therapist who can complete a home assessment.

Promoting Independence and Preventing Accidents

Modification to the home environment can be a key factor in increasing the likelihood of one's parent remaining independent and injury-free in their home and active in their communities as long as they desire. What is a home modification? It is an adaptation to the living environment intended to increase ease of use, safety, security, and independence.

---

[92]   Ibid., 562.

Home modifications can promote independence and prevent accidents. Many persons are living in older structures that are deteriorating to the point that they are hazardous and contribute to falls and injuries; home modifications and repairs can help prevent accidents and falls. The Centers for Disease Control (CDC) suggests that one-third of home accidents can be prevented by modification and repair. Home modifications can enhance comfort, increase safety, prevent injuries, and facilitate ongoing access to community social, recreational, and supportive activities and services. Removing barriers and safety hazards also help reduce the stresses associated with the reduction in physical capabilities as people age.[93] Following a home safety and modification checklist initially or at the slightest change in the health of an older person is noticed can save innumerable time and stress later on. Please refer to the *Home Safety and Modification Checklist* at the end of this chapter. Some home modifications include:

- Lever door handles that operate easily with a push
- Handrails on both sides of staircase and outside steps
- Ramps for accessible entry and exit
- Walk-in shower
- Grab bars in the shower, by the toilet, and by the tub
- Handheld, flexible showerhead
- Lever-handed faucets that are easy to turn on and off
- Sliding shelves and a Lazy Susan in corner cabinet
- C or D ring handles on cabinet doors and drawers for easy gripping

Universal Design

Universal design represents the fact that the changes in who we are and what we can do require a world that is more accommodating to

---

[93]   Ibid., p. 564.

variances in mobility, vision, hearing, cognition, and manual dexterity. Universal design is an approach to creating everyday environments and products that are usable by all people to the greatest extent possible regardless of age or ability, such as the modification of an environment within a home that makes it more accessible for increased independence.[94] Some universal design features include stepless houses, door levers and wider doorways, raised electrical outlets, inferred devices, and wider walk-in showers. A universal house is one that is built from the ground up with universal design features to be labeled as a universal design home.

Why an Assistive Device?

The number of older individuals residing in nursing homes has declined. With the decline of nursing-home population, older adults are living in the community longer. This increase has increased the use of personal assistance devices, also known formally as assistive technology. An assistive device or personal equipment device is an item or product that can be homemade, acquired commercially and modified or customized for a specific individual. The assistive device is one that is used to increase, maintain, or improve functional capacities of an older person.[95] It may be handled, carried, or in some other way be in direct contact with the person. The assistive device may be placed in or attached to the environment or used within it to compensate for or alleviate a potential problem. The inclusion of assistive devices can be very beneficial for the older individual because age-related changes and accompanying diseases often result in functional impairments that lead to a reduction in or loss of independence. By using assistive devices,

---

[94] Taira and Carlson, *Aging in Place: Designing, Adapting, and Enhancing the Home Environment*, 1.

[95] Federal Interagency Forum on Aging-Related Statistics, "2016 Older Americans Key Indicators of Well-Being," August 2016, accessed September 12, 2017, http://agingstats.gov/.

many obstacles can be overcome, even when there has been a decline in physical function.

The following tables offer solutions that can make daily living tasks easier to accomplish. When the parent can do more for themselves, that is success, even if it is with the use of assistive technology devices. When we can empower a loved one to be able to increase their level of independence even in smaller percentages, this is helping them to regain independence and self-esteem. With assistive devices, many everyday tasks and chores can be completed safely, which helps to prevent accidents and promote independence. If an item compensates for functional limitations, it is part of the broad category of assistive technology or assistive devices. Some everyday devices can be very helpful even though they are not marketed as assistive technology.

There are many factors that may influence a person and which should be considered before suggesting or introducing an assistive device. If the person does not understand the need for the device or does not feel it is needed, they will probably not use it. Every day people are required to use new things in their transactions and communications at such places as the bank, the supermarket, and at home. Because of ongoing changes, there is the potential for a parent to feel left out or alienated. One should help their loved one to learn to embrace technology and view it as a tool to improve their quality of life. The following devices are items that can be found relatively easily on the Internet or in any medical supply store. These assistive devices can solve a multitude of problems, and those using them can be taught how to do so in a relatively low time frame. The tables in the following section are only a representation of equipment available and address common problems older adults may experience.

Assistive Technology Device Guide: Common Problems and Assistive Technology Solutions

---

Vision Enhancers

Low vision: Eyeglasses, large-print playing cards, screen magnifier for computer or TV, large-button telephone, bright-colored objects
Blind: Braille books, books on tape, guide cane, screen reader for computer.

| Large-print cards | Portable Video Magnifier | Tactile ink | Large-button phone . |

Living Room

Soft low chair: board under cushion, automatic seat lift, pillow or blanket to raise seat
Swivel and rocking chairs: Device to lock motion
Accessing, reaching, and seeing light switches: Touch-sensitive switches, voice-activated light switches, illuminated wall plates

| Lift chair | Lift seat | Doorknob ext. | Back support |

Bedroom

Rolling bed: Remove wheels, block against wall

Bed to low: Leg extensions, blocks, additional mattress

Getting in/out of bed: portable bed rail

Can't hear clock: Clock with light and vibration attachment

Can't see clock: Large-faced clock, talking talk

Far from bathroom: bedside commode, urinal

Access to clothes: Place clothes in easy-to-reach drawers, shelves, or hangers

Nighttime callers: Bedside phone, cordless phone, intercom

| Talking clock | Bed rail | Lg clock with vibrator | Bedside commode |

Bathroom

Getting in/off toilet: Raised seat, side safety bars, grab bars

Getting in/out of tub: Grab bars, bath/stool chair, transfer bench, handheld shower, and hydraulic lift bath seat

Slipper or wet floors: Nonskid rugs or mats

Shower stool   Safety bars   Nonskid mat   Handheld shower   Long sponge

Telephone

Difficulty reaching: Cordless phone, inform friends to let ring longer, answering machine

Difficulty hearing ring: Ring amplifier, blinking or flashing lights, vibrating ringer

Difficulty holding receiver: Headset, speakerphone, adapted handles

Difficulty hearing other people: Volume control, text telephone (TTY, TDD), headset

Difficulty dialing numbers: Preset memory dial, large buttons and numbers, voice-activated dialing, and all phones the same model with the same preset memory numbers

Voice-activated dialer   TTY   Large-button phone   Phone-alert flasher

Medication

Difficulty opening: Use pill cap opener, have dispensers filled by pharmacist

Difficulty reading label: Use magnifying glass, large print, good lighting

Difficulty remembering medication schedule: Medication organizer, automatic pill dispenser, medication call reminder.

Magnifier   Daily medication keeper   Medication reminder   Talking prescriptions

---

Safety

Difficulty locking doors: Remote-controlled door lock, door wedge
Difficulty opening door and knowing who is there: Automatic door openers, intercom at door, lever doorknob handles, video intercom
Can't hear alarms: Smoke detectors, phone ringing or doorbell: blinking lights, vibrating surfaces.

Flashing smoke detector   Flashing motion detector   Blinking door alert

---

Medication

Difficulty opening: Use pill cap opener, have dispensers filled by pharmacist
Difficulty reading label: Use magnifying glass, large print, good lighting
Difficulty remembering medication schedule: Medication organizer, automatic pill dispenser, medication call reminder.

Magnifier   Daily medication keeper   Medication reminder Talking prescriptions

---

Table 1.0: Assistive technology devices guide[96]

---

[96]   Chart Images from https://www.maxiaids.com/

This chapter contains information that is likely to be new and useful for the caregiver, pastor, and counselor. One should not let all of this information overwhelm and discourage them from investigating it further. Once an individual has finished this book, they can return to this chapter for review. Such a person should be able to discover some useable ideas, home modifications, and assistive technology devices that might be beneficial for their parent. There is a list of companies in the appendices where one can investigate further into different pieces of equipment for finding ways to meet the care receiver's needs. For potential caregivers, the information about home modification, assistive technology, and chronic diseases can be meaningful for future reference if they are unable to use it currently.

Purposeful Thought and Talk through Questions

Here is an opportunity to go deeper into the chapter. By using the discussion questions below, the potential caregiver has an opportunity through self-talk, counseling, or a small group session to discuss scenarios and to think about different options through engaging in conversation. These questions are not designed to be controversial or divisive. There are no right or wrong answers, as each individual and family have different life situations and experiences.

1. How do you think an exercise program could benefit those in your household?
2. What home modifications could be beneficial to your parent?
3. What assistive technology devices could be beneficial to your parent?
4. What are some ways in which a church can help an individual who requires home modifications?
5. From reading this chapter, what are some possible support groups that a church could start?

CHAPTER 6

WHAT WILL YOUR
LEGACY BE?

"A good person leaves an inheritance for their children's children,
but a sinner's wealth is stored up for the righteous"

(PROVERBS 13:22)

What is the first thing that comes to mind when one hears the
names Noah, David, or the boy with the two fish and five loaves?
They left behind something for all of us to learn and grow from, a legacy.
Noah had faith and continued the building of the ark for years, even as
he advanced in age. When the name David is mentioned, one thinks of
David and Goliath, or David, a man after God's own heart. Of course,
there is the boy with the basket of food. He brought and gave all that he
had. Each of these individuals left a mark on our lives, something for
all people to remember. Whether one knew them or not, whether one is
young or old, they left us with something: a legacy. *The American Heritage
Dictionary* defines the term legacy as "something handed down from an
ancestor or a predecessor or the past."[97] One might say that was thousands

---

[97] *The American Heritage Dictionary*, accessed October 17, 2017, https://ahdictionary.
com/word/search.html?q=legacy.

of years ago, and that was then. Those were events that happened before back in the day. This is now and a different time. Is it not? We have the same God now that was back during the times of Noah, David, and the boy with the basket of food. He is also the same God of Adam, Moses, and Paul, who also left legacies of their own. Our God is the same yesterday, today, and forever.

Have you ever thought about what people will say after you pass on? Will they even remember you, if not by your name but by something that you did? Will you hear the words, "Well done, my good and faithful servant"?

Mom loved collecting ceramic chickens and started the hobby after her grandmother gave her several when she was a little girl. She was only nine years old when she started her collection, and it had now grown to well over five hundred, and counting. Her children affectionately called her the chicken lady, and her husband always said, "Stop, stop, we don't have any more room in the house for another chicken." Her friends had dwindled over the years because she rarely left the house and had become so obsessed with collecting chickens. In fact she had missed a lot of her children's activities over the years because she was always busy, looking for none other than another chicken.

"That's a nice story," the minister said as he sat around the table with the family. "But what can you tell me about her? I know she was fifty-seven years old and passed away unexpectedly and had not been to church in a long time. Was she saved?"

The family just looked at the minister as the husband said, "Don't know. We went to church on every holiday and a few times that weren't holidays."

The minister responded, "But what did she do besides collect chickens? Did she belong to any organizations or clubs? Did she read, sew, or like to cook?"

The family looked at each other again, and they all replied almost in unison, "She was the chicken lady. She collected chickens."

Then one of the kids said, "Mom always said she was going to expand her horizons beyond chickens, but she just never did."

The minister sat there, bewildered, wondering how he was going to give the eulogy, and said, "Thank you."

"Legacy, something handed down from an ancestor or a predecessor or from the past."[98] What is your legacy going to be? What are you going to hand down to the younger generations?

Take a minute to complete this quiz. You don't have to actually answer this quiz aloud; just answer the questions to yourself.

1. Name the four wealthiest people in the world.
2. Name the last five Heisman trophy winners.
3. Name the last four winners of the Miss America contest.
4. Name ten people who have won the Nobel or Pulitzer Prize.
5. Name the last five dozen Academy Award winners for the best actor or actress.
6. Name the last five years' worth of World Series winners.

How did you do? Probably not very well, like most people who take this quiz. The point of this exercise is that none of us remember the headliners of yesterday. These are not the second-rate achievers; they are the best in their fields. But the applause dies, awards tarnish, and achievements are soon forgotten. Here's another quiz. See how you do on this one:

1. List five teachers who aided your journey through school.
2. Name three friends who have helped you through a difficult time.
3. Name five people who have taught you something worthwhile.
4. Think of a few people who have made you feel appreciated and special.

---

[98] Ibid.

5. Think of five people with whom you enjoy spending time.
6. Name half a dozen heroes whose stories have inspired you.

The lesson: the people who make a difference in one's life are not the ones with the most credentials, the most money, or the most awards; they are the ones who care.[99]

Don't let Satan say, "You don't have any talent, you are too old, not smart enough, or just too busy." Look at some of those before us. Moses was shy and had a speech impairment. Paul started out as a persecutor of the Jews. The twelve disciples, what a crew they were. Who would have thought that, except for Jesus, a persecutor of God's people, a tax collector, fishermen, and a physician, to name a few, could help bring the Word forward? We all have at least one talent. Are you using yours, or letting it sit idly? "The real talent of life is not being limited to one talent, but in the failure to not use the one talent."[100] God would not call someone to do something if He didn't have the tools for that person to do it. That does not mean one does not have to put effort into what they are doing. They are given the tools; they have to learn how to use them in God's way, not theirs. That is why we have an instructional manual to read: the Bible. When we listen and obey, we succeed in following His will.

We are never too old, and it is never too late to start. Carpe diem, seize the day. It is so aptly written in James 4:14–15: "Why, you do not even know what will happen tomorrow. What is your life? You are a mist that appears for a little while and then vanishes. Instead, you ought to say, 'If it is the Lord's will, we will live and do this or that.'" As a follower of Christ, one has only one life. Therefore we must seize the time appointed to us to use for Him.

With each passing day we are building our legacy. Each of us will leave a legacy behind; our legacy will precede us into eternity. In the book *Legacy: One Life to Live* the author wrote, "What we do in this life will

---

[99] N. A. Very Important People Quiz. N. A. http://www.appleseeds.org/vip_quiz.htm.

[100] Compiled by Snapdragon Editorial Group, *Quiet Moments with God Devotional Journal* (Colorado Springs, CO: Honor Books, 2003), 134.

echo throughout eternity."[101] It is overwhelming when one thinks about the footprint on the future lives we can leave long after we are gone from this world. We are called to make a difference in the world. Our world might be the neighborhood one lives in, where we brings meals to shut-ins. Another person's world might be to be an elected official and bring biblical principles to a crying world. And yet another person's world might be as a missionary across the ocean. One should grow where they are planted and bloom. A simple hello or opening the door for someone could be the nicest thing that has happened to them in days. What if those before us had decided to be complacent? Would we have heard the Word, have a church to attend, or a pastor to preach the message? We have freedoms in this country that people in other parts of the world do not share, such as being able to attend church or talk about God openly. One should plant seeds and let his light shine to help grow them.

How Will You Be Remembered?

It is a stated fact that everyone is going to die. As of now, the mortality rate continues at one out of one. One should start building their legacy today. How do they want to be remembered? What will the hyphen say between their birth and death date? An inventor, Robert Burrows has filed a patent application for a hollow tombstone that features a flat touch screen. When activate the screen will play a video of the dearly departed delivering their final words. Of course, this only works if the person beneath the tombstone has had adequate warning that a final message is called for.[102] People might forget one's name, but not their actions. What if a person were remembered as the lady who read to the students at an elementary school and brought love, compassion, and a light of hope week in and week out? Why not be the person who volunteers at the hospital, the city council member with a Christian perspective, or a small group member?

---

[101] Frank Cox, *Legacy: One Life to Live* (Friendswood, TX: Baxter Press, 2007), 57.

[102] Mikal Keefer, *News You Can Use: 101 Sermon Illustrations* (Loveland, CO: Group Publishing, 2006), 38.

Different Ways for One's Story to Go On

Some ideas that can help an individual begin to leave a legacy:

1. Help at an annual event
2. Run for public office
3. Volunteer at a local school
4. Be a mentor to a local student
5. Visit those in the hospital or nursing home

Teach others about a passion you might have—such as gardening, photography, or cooking—so that they can learn from an experienced person. Start an annual summer BBQ for the neighborhood. Start a community garden and give away the vegetables. One's legacy is limited only by their willingness to get involved.

Putting Your House in Order

Believers have a home for the future. In John 14:2–4, we are promised that, "My Father's house has many rooms; if that were not so, would I have told you that I am going there to prepare a place for you? And if I go and prepare a place for you, I will come back and take you to be with me that you also may be where I am." We are not told the hour, day, or year when we will go to our Father's house, but only that we will. But what about now?

We must get our earthly house in order. Do you want to leave your family confused, fighting, and second-guessing one another? It is difficult to think about wills, estate planning, and funerals because these things are all equated with death, sadness, and loss. Everyone, no matter what their age, should have a will. Estate planning would be even more beneficial. A will is a legal document specifying who the executor of the estate is and how an individual would like the transfer of their property and assets after their death to happen. Estate planning not only includes having a will but also letting family members know how the individual would like their funeral, financial affairs, medical affairs, and other items handled.

An attorney, CPA, or tax advisor who specializes in estate planning can assist in developing an estate plan. They can help in minimizing the taxable portion of one's estate so that their heirs can gain the greatest benefit. This can be an eye-opening experience when an individual starts adding up the value of their estate. Some of the items included when adding up one's assets are their home, investments, retirement savings, and life insurance policies.

The individual knows their desires and how they would like their affairs handled. One's wishes should be in a written legal document to help ensure that they are followed. This is a very stressful time for loved ones; to help alleviate any arguments or displaced feelings, it is paramount that everything is written down so that some of the stress on family members from making decisions can be eliminated. They will not have to labor making a decision because they will already have been made for them. The executor and family will be grateful for their loved one's willingness to have already made many of the decisions so that they can grieve and celebrate his life.

Who Has a Will?

According to *Rocket Lawyer.com*, a website that provides legal services, 57 percent of Americans do not have a will. They also reported that 44 percent of the baby boomers age forty-five to sixty-four years also did not have a will. The survey respondents cited three reasons why they did not have a will: they were procrastinating, held a belief that they did not need one, or they felt the cost of a will was too great. Another alarming statistic is that 35 percent of adults under the age of thirty-five also do not have a will. A will, also known as a "testament," is very important, and everyone should have a current written one. A will voices how one's property will be distributed. If an individual dies without a will, that is known as dying in "interstate." The state will then decide how the property is distributed.[103] Due to the dynamics of individuals, families, and their multiple personalities, if there is not a will present after the death of a parent this can become a fiasco. Add to this the people living together unmarried, along with children from a previous marriage; this has the potential for disaster. A will puts the possessions where and with whom the deceased, also known as a "testator," wanted to receive the property. A will allows the possessions of the deceased to go to the beneficiaries as they desired. A will leaves the testator with a piece of mind and a satisfying fulfillment that their last wishes will be carried out.

What Is Involved with Putting Your House in Order?

There are a variety of publications on the market to help one along their journey of putting their house in order. Some of these are on CDs, and others in a spiral binders or paperback workbooks, with prices ranging anywhere from $15.00 to $100.00. There are pros and cons to each one, but the most important thing is to find one that presents their own information as well as the spouse's information, and is easy to update, orderly, and has additional space in each section for personalized information or notes, which can be invaluable. In the event of an emergency or one's passing, family members are going to require access to a collection of information so that they can proceed with the deceased's final wishes and finalize the estate. Some of the information one will want to be sure of is that the appropriate publications include a section for personal information, available documents and papers, finances, funeral arrangements, and family history. For descriptive and illustrative purposes, the categories from the author's work, *Putting Your House in Order: A Vital Tool for Properly Managing Your Estate*,[104] are being used.

---

[103] N. Craverly, "What to Include in a Simple Will," accessed September 11, 2012, http://www.dummies.com/how-to-/content/what-to-include-in-a-simple-will-html.

[104] Rick C. Caracciolo, *Putting Your House in Order: A Vital Tool for Properly Managing Your Estate* (Oviedo, FL: HigherLife Development Services, 2011).

Quick Reference List

The Quick Reference List is designed to assist a spouse, caregiver, or executor during an extended illness, injury, or death. This section should allow an individual to step in and start locating names, numbers, and addresses immediately without wasting time and energy. This area would list the names and numbers of individuals one would want to be contacted first.

Documents at a Glance

Having these documents organized can be a great time-saver. In this section, one checks only the documents that pertain to them. By indicating if a listed document is an original, a copy, or not available, an individual can save hours of time that may have been spent searching for a document that might not even exist. A person's loved one might need a birth certificate, Social Security card, or a military DD214. Who has the time to look for the brown envelop with an "X" marked on it hidden behind the silverware box in the china cabinet? Maybe the document is in the red shoebox in the closet. What about the blue box under the bed? Indicating which documents exist and where they are located can save time and prevent insurmountable stress on the individual who is searching.

Future Planning

When one hears the words "estate planning," what is the first thing that comes to mind? "I do not have anything of value," or maybe, "I am not wealthy; I only have a few possessions and a little money to leave my family." After one's death, their assets might not be distributed the way they elect. Estate planning enables the transfer of one's assets to their beneficiaries quickly and with minimal negative outcomes; it includes the making of a will or establishing a trust, completing an inventory of their possessions, and talking with the executor and family members. This can be a time to sit with family members and discuss one's financial desires. The individual can inform family members on who they desire to be the executor of their estate; they can discuss medical directives or end-of-life wishes. Consulting an attorney and possibly a CPA will help insure that the documentation has been completed correctly.

Who Has a Will?

"I don't need a will. My family gets along, and everyone knows my wishes." Even though this may be true right now, does this person want to leave their estate and possessions without any direction as to how they should be distributed? When emotions are running high, and grief is bearing down, is it reasonable to think that everyone is going to be thinking with a clear mind? Almost half of all Americans die without having a will. The development of a will can be a relatively inexpensive and easy process. Remember if one does not have a will, the court will intervene and distribute the assets and property in accordance with state law. This distribution may be completed in a manner different from one's wishes. If one does not have a will and there are no apparent heirs, the state could claim the estate.

Executor

The person who executes the instructions in a will is called the executor. The executor should be a trusted person who is of legal age and is willing to assume the responsibility. Usually a spouse, adult child, relative, or trusted friend is asked to be the executor of an estate. One can also have a trust company or an attorney handle the responsibilities, if they so stipulate. The individual preparing their will should be sure to ask if the proposed executor is willing to be the executor of their estate. The responsibilities of an executor can be very time-consuming, stressful, and demanding. Some of the duties that the executor can be called upon to complete are:

- to notify or hire an attorney to assist with the estate, if necessary;
- to file probate papers with the court;
- to inventory assets;
- to set up an estate account and pay debts;
- to notify Social Security of the death;
- to file for life insurance benefits;
- to distribute assets according to the will, when instructed by the court;
- to distribute bequests, gifts, property, and money as outlined in the will and instructed by the court; and
- to obtain death certificates.

Advance Directives

Advance directives are written documents that express to the doctors what kind of treatment one would like to have if they become unable to make medical decisions. The length of the form varies from state to state. It is important that one understands the laws of the state in which they live before completing their advance directives. Further, it would be very helpful to have this completed before they get ill. Federal law at this time requires hospitals, nursing homes, and other institutions that receive Medicare or Medicaid funds to provide written information regarding advance care directives to all patients upon admission.

Living Wills

A living will is an advance directive that comes into effect when a person is terminally ill. A living will does not give someone the opportunity to select another person to make decisions for them, but it allows them to specify the kind of treatment they want in specific situations.

Durable Power of Attorney

A durable power of attorney for health care specifies whom the passing individual has chosen to make medical decisions for them. It is activated when one is unconscious or unable to make medical decisions. It is paramount to choose someone for acting as one's agent who meets the legal requirements of the state. State laws can vary, and most states disqualify anyone under the age of eighteen, the individual's health-care provider, or employees of their health-care provider. When assigning durable power of attorney, one should be sure to let family members and close friends know that there are advance directives and who has been chosen as their agent.

Future Planning

Although death is often a difficult subject to bring up, it is a good idea to discuss these issues with family members to ensure that they understand what one wants in the end. The more communication one has with family members, the easier it will be for them to respect their wishes. Advance directives do not have to be complicated legal documents. They must, however, comply with state laws. It can also be a creditable idea to have a written copy reviewed by one's attorney and physician to be sure that the instructions are clear and legal. Once one has their advance directives finalized, they should consider giving a copy to their family, the durable power-of-attorney agent, and their physician. In the event of an illness or accident, the documents will be required as proof of your desires.

The Funeral

When a loved one dies, family members or close friends are often called upon to make numerous decisions about funeral arrangements. They are under tremendous emotional stress and grief while trying to make choices within a small window of time. There is a way that one can relieve much of the anxiety and stress put upon a loved one by preplanning one's funeral.

When making funeral arrangements whether prepaid or not, one should be sure to keep the Funeral Rule in mind. The Funeral Rule is enforced by the Federal Trade Commission, and requires a funeral director to give the individual itemized prices in person and over the phone. The Funeral Rule also requires funeral directors to give information about their goods and services. Every individual is different and may not want the same type of funeral package. Consumers have the right to choose the funeral goods and services they want with a few exceptions.[105]

Below are a few of the questions one might want to answer and explore to assist when making their final arrangements.

- Is the funeral going to be prepaid or paid at the time of death?
- Do you have military veteran benefits?
- Which funeral home would you like?
- Do you have retirement or burial insurance?
- Where would you like the funeral service to be conducted? Who would you choose to be the one to officiate the service?
- Who would you like to give the eulogy? Which songs would you like sung and by whom?

There is no requirement to answer these types of questions, but it can be a relief for the family to know that they are honoring one's last wishes as they would like. This eliminates the second-guessing and allows the family to grieve their loss, and not to be consumed with making decisions that one can make themselves, such as picking songs or choosing flowers.

Assets

Assets are usually defined as everything that one owns. An asset is a possession that can be given an assessed financial value. Assets come in all kinds of shapes and sizes. If one has particular items that they

---

[105] Federal Trade Commission, The FTC Funeral Rule, accessed September 21, 2017, https://www.consumer.ftc.gov/articles/0300-ftc-funeral-rule.

would like to be given to different individuals, they should discuss this with their attorney for the proper procedures. Because of varying state laws, the attorney can guide the individual so that their wishes might be fulfilled.

Liabilities

Liabilities are usually defined as everything that one owes or is still making payments on. Credit is borrowed money that a person uses to purchase items and then repays within an agreed upon time frame. The average American has four credit cards. One in seven Americans carries more than ten credit cards. We would hope that none of us are like Walter Cavanagh. He at one time had 1,497 valid credit cards, which gave him access to more than $1.7 million in credit. This would be quite a burden for the executor to cancel this number of credit cards.

Family History

An example of a documented family history could be something like Carmine and Marietta, who came from a small city in southern Italy almost one hundred years ago. Their love was strong, and they wanted to be married and live in America. Time was on their side, but patience was not. They wanted to go to America quickly. Carmine had just turned nineteen years of age, and Marietta was only weeks shy of her eighteenth birthday. They had their whole lives in front of them, but they wanted to fulfill their dream then. It had taken them months and months of saving every penny they earned, and they still did not have enough for tickets to America.

The ride across the open seas would take almost two weeks and was costly. They were able to borrow the remaining sum so they could purchase their dream: two tickets to the United States of America. The voyage was long and bumpy. They arrived in America ten days later. They were facing the Statue of Liberty as their ship pulled in to dock. They disembarked the ship and traveled to Ellis Island to begin their dream together. If the information about Carmine and Marietta had not been written down by one of their daughters, it would have been lost forever. One should create a family history by passing along those bits of information and stories that they always meant to share with others.[106]

Another Type of Will

An ethical will is a nonlegal written document in which the individual is asking another individual to carry on a tradition, such as cooking eggs at a watch night service, walking in a yearly Alzheimer's walk, or organizing a family reunion. In other words, this is when other people, usually a family member, are asked to carry on an event or tradition for the individual after their passing. Usually the event is something that the passing individual had been involved in, and this is a way to help carry on their legacy in a nonfinancial manner.

Who Is the Calling For?

The Lord has provided the Christian counselor and pastor with a wonderful opportunity to spread His Word boldly to all of those they meet. There is a need for Christian counselors who want to work or specialize in the area of gerontology or aging. This specialization can be very intense, time-consuming, and can require a significant amount of time outside of the regular counseling office hours. In addition to the regular counseling services, a counselor who is organized and versed in such areas as research, health issues, physiology, assistive technology, Medicare, and home modifications can assist a client and family immensely. Because of the amount of time, effort, and energy involved, senior issues/elderly counseling is not for everyone. Those who enter into this field should have a leading of the Holy Spirit.

---

[106] Caracciolo, *Putting Your House in Order: A Vital Tool for Properly Managing Your Estate.*

As America grays and the elderly population grows at a phenomenal rate over the next twenty years, there will be a need for Christian counselors and pastors who are trained in and understand aging issues.[107] The Christian counselor will inevitably come in contact with a wide range of individuals—differing in age, race, economic circumstances, educational backgrounds, and employment situations—who will all ask for their assistance. This is going to present an opportunity for counselors to use the Word of God, to heal the hurt, the angry, the discouraged, and those with feelings of guilt and hatred that have been festering in their hearts, some for decades. The Christian counselor and pastor can bring the message of salvation. Some counselees will have chosen to ignore the Word because of a hardened heart, while others will now be thirsting for His Word. It is now time for the harvest, "…I tell you, open your eyes and look at the fields! They are ripe for harvest" (John 4:35).

Revisiting the Importance of Forgiveness

Lack of forgiveness is one of the roadblocks that can make a caregiving situation worse. Without true forgiveness there is hostility, anger, resentment, and sometimes health issues. Have you ever felt like you should forgive someone? Did you ever feel like someone should forgive you? Forgiveness, real forgiveness, can take time. The city of Istanbul took eight hundred years. The city was attacked and looted by Crusaders in 1204. During a visit to Greece in 2001, Pope John Paul II apologized publicly for the Roman Catholic Church's support of the Crusaders' campaign. The Pope's apology was formally accepted three years later, on the eight hundredth anniversary of Istanbul's fall, by Orthodox Christian Patriarch Bartholomew.[108] An apology and its acceptance are the beginning steps toward forgiveness… One should start today, not eight hundred years from today. As an individual goes through this process of putting his house in order, they should take time to forgive someone.

---

[107] The United States Census Bureau, accessed May 20, 2017, https://census.gov/.

[108] Keefer, *News You Can Use: 101 Sermon Illustrations*, 49.

It will not be in their will or their list of benefits. It isn't part of the estate property management or funeral service. But one can spend their remaining days benefiting from the peace of forgiveness. They should not wait until there is no time left. Putting their house in order is for everyone, not just seniors. It is something we all should do for our loved ones. We are not promised tomorrow; life can stop abruptly and unexpectedly for any one of us. Just as these pages offer examples of preparing for one's passing, thinking about this can also help one live their final days well. They should do it for themselves; they should do what every family member wishes their loved ones would do: grant forgiveness, receive forgiveness, and accept Jesus as their personal savior.

There Are Many Layers in Caregiving

Living a balanced and life of moderation are the keys to keeping a healthy, positive perspective. "A television comedian once stated something along the line that, if we had our entire lives to live over again we would probably not have the strength."[109] Hopefully one has lived their life to its fullest. Carl Sandburg expressed his feeling about life by saying:

Life is like an onion.
You peel it off
One layer at a time
And sometimes you cry a little.[110]

Caregiving activities are something that continually changes. We all age differently because of genetics, health, and lifestyle. Each day can bring about new challenges and positive memories. As we learn and experience the joys and sorrows of caregiving we should pray without ceasing our joys, sorrows, and thanksgivings. We get out strength from the Lord

---

[109] Ruth Bathauer, *Parent Care: Fear and Loses of the Elderly* (USA: Regal Book, 1984), 31.

[110] Carl Sandburg, "Quotable Quotes," accessed October 1, 2017, https://www.goodreads.com/quotes/134653-life-is-like-an-onion-you-peel-it-off-one.

and He can take us through each day if we allow Him. Regardless of the type of day we are having, respect for our parent is of utmost importance. We all have worth; we are children of the King. Caregiving is not the time to harbor past wrongs and debate parental ills. We may have every reason to be upset with our loved ones' for past wrongs, but if we cannot forgive them maybe we should not be the primary caregiver. When we have anger and unforgiveness in our hearts it shows, even if we have not spoken a word. It can be seen in our actions, decisions, and hearts. It is nearly impossible to give safe and reliable care when we have anger in our hearts. We are not fooling anyone; family, friends, our parents, and ourselves know the anger is there, it is in the air. To be an effective caregiver and example to others who will one day likely be caregivers, we should show them what Christ-likeness is through our words and deeds.

"The Story of the Wooden Bowl"
Author Unknown

A frail old man went to live with his son, daughter-in-law, and
four-year-old grandson.
The old man's hands trembled, his eyesight was blurred, and his
step faltered.
The family ate together at the table. But the elderly grandfather's
shaky hands and failing sight made eating difficult. Peas rolled
off his spoon onto the floor. When he grasped the glass, milk
spilled on the tablecloth.
The son and daughter-in-law became irritated with the mess.
"We must do something about Father," said the son. "I've had
enough of his spilled milk, noisy eating, and food on the floor."
So the husband and wife set a small table in the corner.
There, Grandfather ate alone while the rest of the family enjoyed
dinner without him.
Since Grandfather had broken a dish or two, his food was now
served in a wooden bowl.

When the family glanced in Grandfather's direction, sometimes
he had a tear in his eye as he sat alone.
Still, the only words the couple had for him were sharp
admonitions when he dropped a fork or spilled food.
The four-year-old grandson watched it all in silence.
One evening before supper, the father noticed his son playing
with scrap pieces of wood on the floor.
He asked the child sweetly, "What are you making?"
Just as sweetly, the boy responded, "Oh, I am making a little
bowl for you and Mama to eat your food in when I grow up."
The four-year-old then smiled and went back to work.
The words so struck the parents that they were speechless. Then
tears started to stream down their cheeks. Though no word was
spoken, both knew what must be done.
That evening the husband took Grandfather's hand and gently
led him back to the family table.

For the remainder of his days he ate every meal with the family. And for some reason, neither the husband nor the wife seemed to care any longer when a fork was dropped, milk was spilled, or the tablecloth was soiled.

If one does nothing more than remind those they meet to be respectful and treat the elderly with dignity, they will have solved many concerns and problems. Whether one wants to believe it or not, they will be old one day. How society is instructed to and allowed to treat those in their golden years today is only a taste of what our golden days will have in store for us. When one loses respect for the elderly, they have lost their reverence for life.

Purposeful Thought and Talk through Questions

Here is an opportunity to go deeper into the chapter. By using these questions, one has an opportunity to discuss scenarios and to think about different options through self-talk, counseling, or a small group session. These questions are not designed to be controversial or divisive. There are no right or wrong answers because each individual and family have different life situations and experiences.

1. Are you going to discuss the importance of having a will, advance directives, and medical directives with your parent if they do not have one?
2. Have you discussed your will with the executor and explained to them what your wishes are?
3. Have you discussed with anyone or written out your funeral wishes so that they may be known?
4. Have you considered writing an ethical will after reading about it in this chapter? What would you like your ethical will to be?
5. What new information have you learned from reading this chapter that you plan on implementing immediately?

CHAPTER 7

THIS, THAT, AND THE OTHER:
CONCLUSION

"Trust in the LORD with all your heart and lean not on your own understanding; in all your ways submit to him, and he will make your paths straight"

(PROVERBS 3:5–6)

I f you are still here for these final few pages, you must be serious about learning more about caregiving. As has been demonstrated in previous chapters, caregiving is not for the weak. A caregiver has to make far too many tough decisions to be weak. By now it is clear that being a caregiver is more than fixing lunch or chatting over a cup of coffee while balancing a loved one's checkbook. Caregiving is real life with no holds barred; caregiving is hard work with a blessing. To be a caregiver is to be one who is working hard, but also receiving a blessing. This person's blessing might not be immediate, but it will come at a time and in a form that they will least expect. As a counselor or pastor, you will also be blessed in unknown ways by helping others during their time of need.

Please join with me as we take a few minutes to rewind, move forward, and conclude this pilgrimage. Some of what the preceding chapters have discussed is that we are fearfully and wonderfully made; God has made us into something special, His image. We are the same in the big picture, but we are all different in the smaller things. Each person have their own genealogy, personalities, quirks, and differences. Human beings are as much alike as we are different.

Then we discussed the family and what matters. There are hidden influences in each person that they do not always realize are there. These can include culture, family dynamics, and unresolved personal issues, all of which can be a significant part of decisions one makes as a caregiver or putting all the pieces together when determining if one can be a caregiver.

Moving forward, the analysis then progressed to the responsibilities of the caregiver. This is one of the most important aspects of deciding whether or not to be a caregiver, but unfortunately it is also one of the most forgotten. Can an individual take care of their parents? Yes, they love them, and yes, they want the best for them, but can they live with them every day, day in and day out? And if an individual feels they can live with their loved one, have they thought seriously about there being any unresolved forgiveness, personality differences, caregiver stress, or the availability of respite care and home-care services?

Continuing on, our travels then brought the reader to what most people believe is the only concern: where the parent should live. Most potential caregivers are not aware of all of the other areas we have discussed, and they believe that it is all about housing, or where the potential care receiver will live. This section examined housing options, safety, and what the possibilities for a caregiver and care receiver might be.

Nearing the discussion's end, the chapters delved into assistive technology, health conditions, recreation, medical options, and health care availability. These are all issues that can be glazed over during the caregiver decision-making process, but are a vitally important part of making that final decision to be a caregiver. Being a caregiver has a lot more components than most individuals originally knew. With each component, there are also numerous factors involved in the decision-making process. Each individual and family will have their own mixture of details for their components. Because we are all different, each family has its own specific factors influencing the caregiver components, such as personalities, finances, personal health, and housing, to name a few.

As we traveled down the home stretch of learning about caregiving and deciding whether or not to become the primary caregiver, leaving a legacy, wills, and final wishes were explored. This can be a difficult area for a family to discuss. It is an area where preplanning is done, which can take a tremendous amount of stress off a family. This then allows the loved ones to be less concerned with funeral arrangements and gives them more time to grieve their loss.

This, That, and the Other

So here we are, just steps away from the end of this informational journey. The remaining information has been purposely saved for the end. This information is important, but to keep the focus on each of the main components, it was saved for the end of the book. The following information will not involve a large number of people, but the questions are important; they might make a difference in one's caregiving decision. These are questions that only a caregiver can answer, not research or statistics:

1. If the care receiver has HIV or AIDS, will you or your family feel comfortable caring for them?
2. If your parent has remarried, are you willing to be the caregiver for both individuals? What if your parent passes away first?
3. What if your parent has a lifestyle that you do not agree with, such as one that includes profanity, pornography, or being promiscuous or a homosexual?
4. What if the care receiver smokes, or is addicted to alcohol or drugs?
5. What about being an adult orphan? An adult orphan is an individual who no longer has any living parents or grandparents. They are now the head of the family; they are now the generational leader of the family.

6. Will you leave the same inheritance for all of your children? Will the one who always runs errands, stops by to help, and calls to check on you receive the same inheritance as the others? What about the child who has you move in with them so that they can be your caregiver?

We have undoubtedly traveled down some valleys and reached a few mountaintops during this caregiving journey. Deciding to be a caregiver has to come with a clear understanding of what will be required. Neither an emotional yes nor guilt-contrived comments can be a part of one's decision making. Furthermore these chapters have explored multiple ways to be a caregiver other than having the care receiver move in with the caregiver. One can honor and respect their parents even if they do not move in with them. Just because it is a tough decision does not mean that it is not the best decision for them and their family. It has taken many steps to get this far; this individual is a winner.

Does Your Loved One Know Him?

I would like to close with one parting question for the potential caregiver: has your parent or loved one accepted Jesus as their personal Savior? Think about this for a minute. If your loved one has not accepted Jesus as their Savior, do you not think they should? Just as one has been concerned about where the parent will reside, now should they not be even more concerned about where the parent will reside for all eternity? If one does not feel comfortable presenting the gospel to their parents, they should find a friend or pastor to do it for them. All that one can do is present the gospel to them; it is their choice if they do not accept. Do not let another day pass by without presenting them the opportunity to accept Jesus as their Savior, just as He showed us undeserving mercy and took the nails in His hands for us, and just as the love of Jesus has no depth, no height, or no measurement. Let them have the opportunity to know that the love of Jesus has no end.

Abbreviations

ADLs ....activities of daily living

ADON..assistant director of nursing

CNA...certified nursing assistant

COTA .... certified occupational therapy assistant

DON... director of nursing

LTC...long-term care facility

OT.. occupational therapist

PT ....physical therapist

PTA... physical therapy assistant

ROM.. range on motion

RT ....respiratory therapist

SLP... speech language pathologist

SNF..skilled nursing facility

Glossary

Abuse (personal). It is when another person does something on purpose that causes another person mental or physical harm or pain.

Activities of daily living. Activities of daily living (ADL's) includes the self-maintenance task of dressing, grooming, feeding, dressing, eating, mobility, communication, socialization, and sexual expression.

Admitting physician. This is physician responsible for admitting a patient to a hospital or other inpatient health facility.

Advance directives. It is written document stating how you want medical decisions to be made if you lose the ability to make them for yourself. It may include a living will and a durable power of attorney for health care.

Assisted living. This is a type of living arrangement in which personal-care services such as meals, housekeeping, transportation, and assistance with activities of daily living are available as needed to people who still live on their own in a residential facility. In most cases, the "assisted living" residents pay a regular monthly rent. Then they typically pay additional fees for the services they get.

Care plan. This is a written plan for your care. It tells what services you will get to reach and keep your best physical, mental, and social well-being.

Caregiver. This is person who helps care for someone who is ill, disabled, or aged. Some caregivers are relatives or friends who volunteer their help. Some people provide caregiving services for a cost.

Durable power of attorney. It is legal document that enables you to designate another person, called the attorney-in-fact, to act on your behalf, in the event you become disabled or incapacitated.

Geriatrics. It is the study of all aspects of aging, including the physiological, psychological, economic, and sociological problems of the elderly.[111]

Home health care. It is a limited, part-time, or intermittent skilled nursing care and home health aide services, physical therapy, occupational therapy, speech-language therapy, medical-social services, durable medical equipment (such as wheelchairs, hospital beds, oxygen, and walkers), medical supplies, and other services.

Homebound. This normally means one is unable to leave the home unassisted. To be homebound means that leaving home takes considerable and taxing effort. A person may leave home for medical treatment or short, infrequent absences for nonmedical reasons, such as a trip to the barber or to attend religious services. A need for adult day care does not keep you from getting home health care.

Hospice. Hospice is a special way of caring for people who are terminally ill, and for their family. This care includes physical care and counseling. Hospice care is covered under Medicare Part A (Hospital Insurance).

Living wills. It is legal document, also known as a medical directive or advance directive. It states your wishes regarding life support or other medical treatment in certain circumstances, usually when death is imminent.

Long-term care survey. The long-term care survey is an evaluation process by which a nursing home is inspected and evaluated to determine if they are meeting state and federal regulations.

---

[111] Haru Hirama, *Occupational Therapy Assistant: A Primer* (Baltimore, MD: Chess Publication, 1990), 285.

Medicaid. It is a joint federal and state program that helps with medical costs for some people with low incomes and limited resources. Medicaid programs vary from state to state, but most health-care costs are covered if you qualify for both Medicare and Medicaid.

Medicare. The federal health insurance program for people sixty-five years of age or older, certain younger people with disabilities, and people with end-stage renal disease (permanent kidney failure with dialysis or a transplant, sometimes called ESRD).

Nursing home. A nursing home is a residence that provides a variety of services, such as a room, meals, recreational activities, assistance with activities of daily living, and protection/supervision to residents. Nursing homes are licensed by the state and are required to follow state and federal regulations. Some nursing homes specialize in areas such as Alzheimer's disease, pain management, incontinence training, and cardiac rehab.

Occupational therapy. Occupational therapy is a rehabilitation specialty that is provided by a licensed individual. The occupational therapist works with individuals with varying disabilities. Some of the areas the therapist may help the individual regain function of are self-feeding, oral hygiene, upper body strengthening, dressing/bathing skills, visual/perceptual coordination, splinting, and adaptive equipment.

Ombudsman. The ombudsman visits the nursing home on a regular basis. It is their job to mediate disputes, investigate complaints, and be an advocate for residents.

Physical therapy. It is a rehabilitation specialty that is provided by a licensed individual. The physical therapist may work with an individual depending upon the diagnosis to help them regain functional abilities in walking, getting in/out of bed, strength, balance, gross motor skills, endurance, and improve safety skills.

Range of motion. It is the arc of motion that joints pass through. ROM measurements can help a therapist determine appropriate treatment goals and current range of motion degrees.

Respiratory services. These are services provided to an individual who might have breathing disorders or breathing difficulties. Some of the areas respiratory services are provided are aerosol therapy, delivering oxygen therapy, and exercises in breathing retraining.

Speech language pathologist. This is a rehabilitation specialty that is provided by a licensed individual. The speech language pathologist assists individuals with varying disabilities. Some of the areas they assist on are individuals who have difficulties in chewing, swallowing, speech, comprehension, communications, and memory loss.

REFERENCES

"10 Superhuman Feats of Ordinary People." Accessed December 26, 2017. http://www.learning-mind.com/ superhuman-feats-of-ordinary-people/.

"Advance Directives." Accessed October 15, 2017. http://www.caringinfo.org/i4a/pages/index. cfm?pageid=1&activateFull=false.

The American Heritage Dictionary. Accessed October 17, 2018. https://ahdictionary.com/word/search.html?q=legacy.

Anderson, Neil T. and Terry E. Zuehlke. *Christ-Centered Therapy.* (Grand Rapids, MI: Zondervan Publishing House, 2002).

Bathauer, Ruth. *Parent Care: Fear and Loses of the Elderly.* (USA: Regal Book, 1984).

Beerman, Susan and Judith Rappaport. *Eldercare 911: The Caregiver's Complete Handbook for Making Decisions.* (Amherst, NY, 2002).

Biegel, Leonard. *Physical Fitness and the Older Person: A Guide to Exercise for Health Care Professionals.* (Rockville, MD: Aspens Systems Corporation, 1984).

Bingham, Caroline. *The Human Body.* (New York, New York: DK Publishers, 2003).

Bonder, Bette R. and Marilyn B. Wagner. *Functional Performance in Older Adults.* (Philadelphia, PA: F. A. Davis Company, 1994).

Buttrick, David. *Graying Gracefully: Preaching to Older Adults.* (Louisville, KY: Westminster John Knox Press, 1997).

Caracciolo, Rick C. *Putting Your House in Order: A Vital Tool for Properly Managing Your Estate.* (Oviedo, FL: HigherLife Development Services, 2011).

Craverly, N. "What to Include in a Simple Will." Accessed September 11, 2012. http://www.dummies.com/how-to-/ content/what-to-include-in-a-simple-will-html.

Christenson, Margaret A. *Aging in the Designed Environment.* (Binghamton, New York: Haworth Press, 1990).

Davis, Ruth. *The Nursing Home Handbook.* (Holbrook, MA: Adams Media Corporation, 2000).

Federal Interagency Forum on Aging-Related Statistics. "Older Americans 2004: Key Indicators of Well-Being." November 1, 2004. Accessed May 1, 2017. https://agingstats.gov/docs/ PastReports/2004/OA2004.pdf.

Federal Interagency Forum on Aging-Related Statistics. "2016 Older Americans Key Indicators of Well-Being." August 2016. Accessed September 12, 2017. http://agingstats.gov/.

Federal Interagency Forum on Aging-Related Statistics. "Older Americans 2016 Key Indicators of Well-Being." August 2016. Accessed December 14, 2017. http://agingstats.gov/docs/ LatestReport/Older-Americans-2016-Key-Indicators-of- WellBeing.pdf.

Federal Trade Commission. "The FTC Funeral Rule." Accessed September 21, 2017. https://www.consumer.ftc.gov/ articles/0300-ftc-funeral-rule.

Frankel, Victor E. *Man's Search for Meaning.* (Boston, MA: Beacon Press, 1962).

Gelhaus, L. "Boomers Prefer Aging at Home," *Provider Magazine* 30 (2004).

Gentzler, Richard. *Aging and Ministry in the 21st Century.* (Nashville, TN: Discipleship Resources, 2008).

Guinness, Alma E., ed. *ABCs of the Human Body.* (USA: Reader's Digest, 1987).

Henry, Matthew. "The Care He Took of His Mother." Accessed November 1, 2017. https://www.wordsearchbible.com.

Hiavochee, Joe P. *Keeping Young and Living Longer.* (Los Angeles, CA: Sherbourne Press, 1972).

Hirama, Haru. *Occupational Therapy Assistant: A Primer.* (Baltimore, MD: Chess Publication, 1990).

Holmes, T. H. and T. H. Rahe. "The Social Adjustment Rating Scale," *Journal of Psychosomatic Research*, 11 no. 2 (August 1967).

Houston, James M. and Michael Parker. *A Vision for the Aging Church.* (Downers Grove, Il: IVP Academic, 2011).

Keefer, Mikal. *News You Can Use: 101 Sermon Illustrations.* (Loveland, CO: Group Publishing, 2006).

Lazarus, Richard. "The Holmes and Rahe Test Scale." July 26, 2013. Accessed November 10, 2017. http://slipstream6011719.word-press.com/tag/richard-lazarus/.

Littauer, Florence. *Your Personality Tree.* (Waco, TX: Word Books, 1986).

Lynch, Eleanor W. and Marci J. Hanson. *Developing Cross-Cultural Competence.* (Baltimore, MD: Paul H. Brookes Publishing Company, 1992).

Margaret, A. and Christianson. *Aging in the Designed Environment.* (Binghamton, NY: Haworth Press, 1990).

"Marital Status and Living Arrangements." Accessed November 17, 2017. http://www.census.gov/hhes/families/data/cps2016.

McMillen, S. I. *None of These Diseases.* (Grand Rapids, MI: Spire Books, 1963).

Mezey, Mathy. *The Encyclopedia of Elder Care.* (Amherst, NY: Prometheus Books, 2004).

Mind Tools Content Team. "The Holmes and Rahe Stress Scale." Accessed October 25, 2017. https://www.mindtools.com/pages/article/newTCS_82.htm?utm_term=holmes+rahe+stress+scale&utm_content=p1-main-3-title&utm_medium=sem&utm_source=msn_s&utm_campaign=-adid-9916ce56-9147-4f81-9ccd-8f488aa4b406-0-ab_msb_ocode-22837&ad=semD&an=msn_s&am=broad&q=holmes+rahe+stress+scale&o=22837&qsrc=999&l=sem&askid=9916ce56-9147-4f81-9ccd-8f488aa4b406-0-ab_msb.

McLean, Leslie and Wilburn Clouse. "Stress and Burnout: An Organizational Synthesis." December 1, 1990. Accessed June 21, 2017. https://files.eric.ed.gov/fulltext/ED341140.pdf.

McLeod, Saul. "Type A Personality." 2017. Accessed August 1, 2017. https://www.simplypsychology.org/personality-a.html.

Merrill, Deborah M. *Caring for Elderly Parents*. (Westport, CT: Auburn House, 1997).

Northern, Vicki Moore. "Family Caregiving of the Elderly Parent," *Journal of Family Ministry* 16, no. 1 (Spring 2002).

Novak, Jill. "The Six Living Generations in America." November/April. Accessed June 16, 2017. http://www.marketingteacher.com/the-six-living-generations-in-america/.

N. A. "Old Age." 2004. Accessed February 22, 2005. http://www.realtime.net/wdoud/topics/oldage.html.

N. A. "Very Important People Quiz." N. A. http://www.appleseeds.org/vip_quiz.htm.

Sandburg, Carl. Quotable Quotes. Accessed October 1, 2017. https://www.goodreads.com/quotes/134653-life-is-like-an-onion-you-peel-it-off-one.

Schomp, Virginia. *Aging Parent Handbook: The Baby Boomer Dilemma*. (New York, NY: Harper Collins Publishers, 1997).

Shelly, Susan. *When It's Your Turn: Grown Children Caring for Aging Parents*. (United States of America: Barnes & Noble, 2003).

Silverstein, Shel. "The Little Boy and the Old Man." Accessed December 1, 2017. https://www.familyfriendpoems.com/poem/the-little-boy-and-old-man-by-shel-silverstein.

Smith, Penny, ed. *First Human Body Encyclopedia.* (New York, New York: DK Publishing, 2003).

Snapdragon Editorial Group. *Quiet Moments with God Devotional Journal.* (Colorado Springs, CO: Honor Books, 2003).

Stoppelenburg, Arianne. "The Effects of Advance Care Planning on End of Life Care." September 1, 2014. Accessed January 2, 2018. https://eapcnet.wordpress.com/2014/09/01/the-effects-of-advance-care-planning-on-end-of-life-care/.

Taira, Ellen D. and Jodi Carlson. *Aging in Place: Designing, Adapting, and Enhancing the Home Environment.* (Binghamton, NY: Haworth Press, 2002).

The United States Census Bureau. Accessed May 1, 2017. https://www.census.gov/prod/2014pubs/p20-574.pdf.

The United States Census Bureau. Accessed May 20, 2017. https://census.gov/.

United States Government. "Older Americans 2004 Key Indicators of Well-Being." August 2016. Accessed September 20, 2016. https://agingstats.gov/docs/PastReports/2004/OA2004.pdf.

United States Government. "Older Americans 2004 Key Indicators of Well-Being." August 2016. Accessed September 20, 2016. https://agingstats.gov/docs/LatestReport/Older-Americans-.

United States Government. "Older Americans 2016 Key Indicators of Well-Being." August 2016. Accessed September 20, 2016. https://agingstats.gov/docs/LatestReport/Older-Americans-2016-Key-Indicators-of-WellBeing.pdf.

United States Government. National Center for Health Statistics. Last modified May 3, 2017. Accessed September 17, 2017. https://www.cdc.gov/nchs/fastats/nursing-home-care.htm.

Unknown. "Why We Get Old," *Harvard Health Letter*. October 1992.

Wood, Beulla. "A Theology of the Generations: Do People Still Risk Feudalism in the Family?" *Priscilla Papers* 23, no. 3 (Summer 2008).

APPENDICES

Appendix A

The Six Living Generations' Generational Differences

There are six living generations in the United States. Each of these six generational groups of people are distinct from each other. Respectively, each generation has their own distinct likes, dislikes, and particular characteristics. Each generation has grown up and lived through similar experiences and societal influences and changes. An individual's age should not be the only factor used when determining individual characteristics. Their age is a guide to discover the similarities, the likes and dislikes that they might have with their generational group.[112]

GI Generation:

- Born 1901–1926
- Children of the WWI generation and fighters in WWII, young in the Great Depression…all leading to strong models of teamwork to overcome and progress
- Their depression was the *great one*; their war was the *big one*; their prosperity was the legendary *happy days*.

---

[112] Jill Novak, "The Six Living Generations in America," November/April, accessed June 16, 2017, http://www.marketingteacher.com/the-six-living-generations-in-america/.

- They saved the world and then built a nation.
- They are the assertive and energetic doers.
- Excellent team players
- Community-minded
- Strongly interested in personal morality and near-absolute standards of right and wrong
- Strong sense of personal civic duty, which means they vote
- Marriage is for life, divorce and having children out of wedlock were not accepted
- Strong loyalty to jobs, groups, schools, and the like
- There was no "retirement"; you worked until you died or couldn't work anymore.
- The labor-union-spawning generation
- "Use it up, fix it up, make it do, or do without."
- Avoid debt…save and buy with cash.
- Age of radio and air flight; they were the generation that remembers life without airplanes, radio, and TV.
- Most of them grew up without modern conveniences like refrigerators, electricity, and air conditioning.
- Sometimes called the greatest generation

Mature/Silent Generation:

- Born 1927–1945
- Went through their formative years during an era of suffocating conformity, but also during the postwar happiness: Peace! Jobs! Suburbs! Television! Rock 'n Roll! Cars! *Playboy* magazine!
- Korean and Vietnam War generation
- The first hopeful drumbeats of civil rights!
- Pre-feminism women; women stayed home generally to raise children; if they worked it was only certain jobs like teacher, nurse, or secretary

- Men pledged loyalty to the corporation; once you got a job, you generally kept it for life.
- The richest, most free-spending retirees in history
- Marriage is for life; divorce and having children out of wedlock were not accepted.
- In grade school, the gravest teacher complaints were about passing notes and chewing gum in class.
- They are avid readers, especially newspapers.
- "Retirement" means to sit in a rocking chair and live your final days in peace.
- The big-band/swing music generation
- Strong sense of trans-generational common values and near-absolute truths
- Disciplined, self-sacrificing, and cautious

Baby Boomers Generation:

Baby boomers are the demographic of people who were born just after the Second World War; this would give the baby boomer generation an approximate date of between 1946 and 1964. World War Two ended in 1945, and as a rule of thumb, baby boomers are the children who are born as the war ended, as families settled down again.

- Born between 1946 and 1964. Two sub-sets: the save-the-world revolutionaries of the '60s and '70s, and the party-hardy career climbers (yuppies) of the '70s/'80s
- The "me" generation
- "Rock and roll" music generation
- Ushered in the free love and societal, "nonviolent" protests that triggered violence
- Self-righteous and self-centered
- Buy it now and use credit.

- Too busy for much neighborly involvement, yet strong desires to reset or change the common values for the good of all
- Even though their mothers were generally housewives, responsible for all child rearing, women of this generation began working outside the home in record numbers, thereby changing the entire nation, as this was the first generation to have their own children raised in a two-income household, where mom was not omnipresent.
- The first TV generation
- The first divorce generation, where divorce was beginning to be accepted as a tolerable reality
- Began accepting homosexuals
- Optimistic, driven, team-oriented
- Envision technology and innovation as requiring a learning process
- Tend to be more positive about authority, hierarchal structure, and tradition
- One of the largest generations in history, with 77 million people
- Their aging will change America almost incomprehensibly; they are the first generation to use the word "retirement" to mean being able to enjoy life after the children have left home. Instead of sitting in a rocking chair, they go skydiving, exercise, and take up hobbies, which increases their longevity.
- The American youth culture that began with them is now ending with them, and their activism is beginning to reemerge.

Generation X:

- Born between 1965 and 1980*
- The "latch-key kids" grew up street-smart but isolated, often with divorced or career-driven parents. Latch-key came from the house key kids wore around their necks, because they would go home from school to an empty house.

- Entrepreneurial
- Very individualistic
- Government and big business mean little to them.
- Want to save the neighborhood, not the world
- Feel misunderstood by other generations
- Cynical of many major institutions, which failed their parents, or them, during their formative years and are therefore eager to make marriage work and "be there" for their children
- Don't "feel" like a generation, but they are
- Raised in the transition phase of written-based knowledge to digital-knowledge archives; most remember being in school without computers and then after the introduction of computers in middle school or high school
- Desire a chance to learn, explore, and make a contribution
- They tend to commit to self rather than an organization or specific career. This generation averages seven career changes in their lifetime; it was not normal to work for a company for life, unlike previous generations.
- Society and thus individuals are envisioned as disposable
- AIDS begins to spread and is first lethal infectious disease in the history of any culture on earth, which was not subjected to any quarantine
- Beginning obsession of individual rights prevailing over the common good, especially if it is applicable to any type of minority group
- Raised by the career- and money-conscious boomers amidst the societal disappointment over governmental authority and the Vietnam War
- School problems were about drugs
- Late to marry (after cohabitation) and quick to divorce…many single parents
- Into labels and brand names

- Want what they want and want it now but struggling to buy, and most are deeply in credit card debt
- It has been researched that they may be conversationally shallow because relating consists of shared time watching video movies, instead of previous generations.
- Short on loyalty and wary of commitment; all values are relative…must tolerate all peoples
- Self-absorbed and suspicious of all organizations
- Survivors as individuals
- Cautious, skeptical, unimpressed with authority, self-reliant

Generation Y/Millennium:

- Born between 1981* and 2000.
- Dubbed the "9/11 Generation," "Echo Boomers," America's next great generation brings a sharp departure from Generation X.
- They are nurtured by omnipresent parents, optimistic, and focused.
- Respects authority
- Falling crime rates, falling teen pregnancy rates, but with school safety problems; they have to live with the thought that they could be shot at school, and they learned early that the world is not a safe place.
- They schedule everything.
- They feel enormous academic pressure.
- They feel like a generation and have great expectations for themselves.
- They prefer digital literacy, as they grew up in a digital environment. They have never known a world without computers! They get all their information and most of their socialization from the Internet.
- Prefer to work in teams

- With unlimited access to information, tend to be assertive with strong views
- Envision the world as a 24/7 place; want fast and immediate processing
- They have been told over and over again that they are special, and they expect the world to treat them that way.
- They do not live to work; they prefer a more relaxed work environment with a lot of hand-holding and accolades.

Generation Z/Boomlets:

- Born after 2001*
- In 2006, there were a record number of births in the US and 49 percent of those born were Hispanic. This will change the American melting pot in terms of behavior and culture. The number of births in 2006 far outnumbered the start of the baby boom generation, and they will easily be a larger generation.
- Since the early 1700s, the most common last name in the US was "Smith," but not anymore. Now it is Rodriguez.
- There are two age groups right now:
  - (a) Tweens
  - (a1) Age eight to twelve years old
  - (a2) There will be an estimated 29 million tweens by 2009.
  - (a3) $51 billion is spent by tweens every year, with an additional $170 billion spent by their parents and family members directly for them.
  - (b)Toddler/elementary school age
- 61 percent of children, eight to seventeen, have televisions in their rooms
- 35 percent have video games
- 14 percent have DVD players
- 4 million will have their own cell phones. They have never known a world without computers and cell phones.

- The have eco-fatigue. They are actually tired of hearing about the environment and the many ways we have to save it.
- With the advent of computers and web-based learning, children leave behind toys at younger and younger ages. It's called KGOY-kids growing older younger, and many companies have suffered because of it, most recognizable is Mattel, the maker of Barbie dolls. In the 1990s, the average age of a child in their target market was ten years old, and in 2000, it dropped to three years old. As children reach the age of four and five, old enough to play on the computer, they become less interested in toys and begin to desire electronics, such as cell phones and video games.

They are savvy consumers, and they know what they want and how to get it, and they are oversaturated with brands.[113]

---

[113] Ibid.

Appendix B

Exhibit 1: Senior Housing Guide Checklist

*On-site visitation checklist

Name of Senior Home: _____

Date of Visit: _____

Basic Information

- ☐ The senior home is Medicare-certified.
- ☐ The senior home is Medicaid-certified.
- ☐ The senior home has the level of care needed (e.g. skilled, custodial), and a bed is available.
- ☐ The senior home has special services if needed in a separate unit (e.g. dementia, ventilator, or rehabilitation), and a bed is available.
- ☐ The senior home is located close enough for friends and family to visit.

Resident Appearance

- ☐ Residents are clean, appropriately dressed for the season or time of day, and well groomed.

Senior Home Living Spaces

- ☐ The senior home is free from overwhelming unpleasant odors.
- ☐ The senior home appears clean and well kept.
- ☐ The temperature in the senior home is comfortable for residents.

☐ The senior home has good lighting. Noise levels in the dining room and other common areas are comfortable.

☐ Smoking is not allowed or may be restricted to certain areas of the senior home.

☐ Furnishings are sturdy, yet comfortable and attractive.

Staff

☐ The relationship between the staff and the residents appears to be warm, polite, and respectful.

☐ All staff wear name tags. Staff knock on the door before entering a resident's room and refer to residents by name.

☐ The senior home offers a training and continuing education program for all staff.

☐ The senior home does background checks on all staff.

☐ The guide on your tour knows the residents by name and is recognized by them.

☐ There is a full-time Registered Nurse (RN) in the nursing home and the senior home at all times, other than the Administrator or Director of Nursing.

☐ The same team of nurses and Certified Nursing Assistants (CNAs) work with the same resident 4 to 5 days per week.

☐ CNAs work with a reasonable number of residents.

☐ CNAs are involved in care planning meetings.

☐ There is a full-time social worker on staff.

☐ There is a licensed doctor on staff. Is he or she there daily? Can he or she be reached at all times?

☐ The senior home's management team has worked together for at least one year.

Residents' Rooms

- ☐ Residents may have personal belongings and/or furniture in their rooms.
- ☐ Each resident has storage space (closet and drawers) in his or her room. Each resident has a window in his or her bedroom.
- ☐ Residents have access to a personal telephone and television.
- ☐ Residents have a choice of roommates.
- ☐ Water pitchers can be reached by residents.
- ☐ There are policies and procedures to protect resident's possessions.
- ☐ Hallways, Stairs, Lounges, and Bathrooms Exits are clearly marked.
- ☐ There are quiet areas where residents can visit with friends and family.
- ☐ The senior home has smoke detectors and sprinklers.
- ☐ All common areas, resident rooms, and doorways are designed for wheelchair use.
- ☐ Are there handrails in the hallways and grab bars in the bathrooms?

Menus and Food

- ☐ Residents have a choice of food items at each meal.
  (Ask if your favorite foods are served.)
- ☐ Nutritious snacks are available upon request.
- ☐ Staff help residents eat and drink at mealtimes if help is needed.

Activities

- ☐ Residents, including those who are unable to leave their rooms, may choose to take part in a variety of activities.

- ☐ The senior home has outdoor areas for resident use and staff help residents go outside.
- ☐ The senior home has an active volunteer program.

Safety and Care

- ☐ The senior home has an emergency evacuation plan and holds regular fire drills.
- ☐ Residents get preventive care, like a yearly flu shot, to help keep them healthy.
- ☐ Residents may still see their personal doctors.
- ☐ The senior home has an arrangement with a nearby hospital for emergencies.
- ☐ Care plan meetings are held at times that are convenient for residents and family members to attend whenever possible.
- ☐ The senior home has corrected all deficiencies (failure to meet one or more Federal or State requirements) on the previous state inspection report.

Additional Comments:

Exhibit 2: Care Facility Profile

*Initial telephone interview or mail to care facility to complete and return.

Care Facility:

- ☐ Care Facility Name: _____
- ☐ Address: _____
- ☐ City: _____ Zip Code: _____
- ☐ County_____
- ☐ Phone: ()_____ Fax: ()_____
- ☐ E-Mail: _____

Care Facility Staff:

- ☐ Administrator: _____
- ☐ Assistant Administrator_____
- ☐ Admissions Coordinator: _____
- ☐ DON: _____

Payment Types Accepted:

*Please check all that apply.

- ☐ Medicaid
- ☐ Medicare
- ☐ Private Pay
- ☐ Veterans
- ☐ Private Insurance

Health Services Offered:

*Please check all that apply.

- ☐ Skilled Nursing Care
- ☐ Alzheimer/Dementia Care Unit
- ☐ Private Pay Rooms
- ☐ Incontinence Program
- ☐ Pain Management Program
- ☐ Physical Therapy
- ☐ Occupational Therapy
- ☐ Speech/Language Therapy
- ☐ Stroke Rehabilitation Program
- ☐ Wound Care
- ☐ Podiatry Services
- ☐ Recreational Therapy
- ☐ Medical Director
- ☐ 24 Hour Nursing Care
- ☐ Hospice Services
- ☐ Sub-Acute Unit
- ☐ Pharmacy
- ☐ Respiratory Therapy
- ☐ Dietitian

Care Facility Services/Features:

*Please check all that apply.

- ☐ Dining Room
- ☐ Day Room
- ☐ TV Room
- ☐ Beauty/Barber Shop
- ☐ Library

- ☐ Worship Services
- ☐ Laundry Services
- ☐ Outdoor/Patio Area
- ☐ Activities Room
- ☐ Room Visitations
- ☐ Special Activities
- ☐ Movies
- ☐ Activities/Games
- ☐ Crafts
- ☐ Intergenerational Programs
- ☐ Exercise Group
- ☐ Holiday Activities

Mission/Purpose:

_____

_____

_____

_____

_____

Optional-Narrative:

*Please list all those features, services, or activities that make this facility "Special."

_____

_____

_____

_____

_____

Exhibit 3: Emergency Call Contact List

*In an emergency, call 911

☐ Family members – names to contact in an emergency

    a) Name:

        Telephone number:

    b) Name:

        Telephone number:

☐ Physicians – name, medical specialty, and telephone

    a) Name:

        Medical specialty:
        Telephone number:

    b) Name:

        Medical specialty:
        Telephone number:

    c) Name:

        Medical specialty:
        Telephone number:

    d) Name:

        Medical specialty:
        Telephone number:

☐ Pharmacy – name and telephone number

    a) Name:

    Telephone number:

☐ Friends and neighbors – name and telephone number

    a) Name:

    Telephone number:

    b) Name:

    Telephone number:

    c) Name:

    Telephone number:

    d) Name:

    Telephone number:

☐ Elder Care Attorney – name and telephone number

    a) Name:

    Telephone number:

Exhibit 4: Georgia Living Will*

Living will, made this day of month year.

I, being of sound mind, willfully and voluntarily make known my desire that my life shall not be prolonged under the circumstances set forth below and do declare:

1. If at any time I should (check each option desired):
   - ( ) have a terminal condition,
   - ( ) become in a coma with no reasonable expectation of regaining consciousness, or
   - ( ) become in a persistent vegetative state with no reasonable expectation of regaining significant cognitive function, as defined in and established in accordance with the procedures set forth in paragraphs (2), (9), and (13) of Code Section 31-32-2 of the Official Code of Georgia Annotated, I direct that the application of life-sustaining procedures to my body be withheld or withdrawn and that I be permitted to die.

With regard to artificially supplied nutrition and hydration, I direct that:

(check the option desired)
( ) artificial nutrition be provided.
( ) artificial nutrition be withheld or withdrawn.

(check the option desired)
( ) artificial hydration be provided.
( ) artificial hydration be withheld or withdrawn.

Other directions:
2. In the absence of my ability to give directions regarding the use

* *www.caringinfo.com*

of such life-sustaining procedures, it is my intention that this living will shall be honored by my family and physician(s) as the final expression of my legal right to refuse medical or surgical treatment and accept the consequences from such refusal;

3. I understand that I may revoke this living will at any time;
4. I understand the full import of this living will, and I am at least 18 years of age and am emotionally and mentally competent to make this living will; and
5. If am a female and I have been diagnosed as pregnant, I want this living will to be carried out despite my pregnancy.   (initial)

Signed

City

County

State of Residence

I hereby witness this living will and attest that:

(1) The declarant is personally known to me and I believe the declarant to be at least 18 years of age and of sound mind;
(2) I am at least 18 years of age;
(3) To the best of my knowledge, at the time of the execution of this living will, I:

    a) Am not related to the declarant by blood or marriage;
    b) Would not be entitled to any portion of the declarant's estate by any will or by operation of law under the rules of descent and distribution of this state;
    c) Am not the attending physician of declarant or an employee

of the attending physician or an employee of the hospital or skilled nursing facility in which declarant is a patient;

d) Am not directly financially responsible for the declarant's medical care; and

e) Have no present claim against any portion of the estate of the declarant;

(4) Declarant has signed this document in my presence as above instructed, on the date above first shown.

Witness

Address

Witness

Address

Additional witness required when living will is signed by a patient in a hospital or skilled nursing facility. I hereby witness this living will and attest that I believe the declarant to be of sound mind and to have made this living will willingly and voluntarily.

Witness

(Medical director of skilled nursing facility or staff physician not participating in care of the patient, or chief of the hospital medical staff or staff physician or hospital designee not participating in care of the patient.)

Courtesy of Caring Connections
1700 Diagonal Road, Suite 625, Alexandria, VA 22314
www.caringinfo.org. 800/658-8898

@ 2005 National Hospice and Palliative Care Organization

Exhibit 5: Georgia Statutory Short Form Durable Power of Attorney for Health Care*

(A reminder from National Hospice and Palliative Care Organization): NOTICE: THE PURPOSE OF THIS POWER OF ATTORNEY IS TO GIVE THE PERSON YOU DESIGNATE (YOUR AGENT) BROAD POWERS TO MAKE HEALTH CARE DECISIONS FOR YOU, INCLUDING POWER TO REQUIRE, CONSENT TO, OR WITHDRAW ANY TYPE OF PERSONAL CARE OR MEDICAL TREATMENT FOR ANY PHYSICAL OR MENTAL CONDITION AND TO ADMIT YOU TO OR DISCHARGE YOU FROM ANY HOSPITAL, HOME, OR OTHER INSTITUTION; BUT NOT INCLUDING PSYCHOSURGERY, STERILIZATION, OR INVOLUNTARY HOSPITALIZATION OR TREATMENT COVERED BY TITLE 37 OF THE OFFICIAL CODE OF GEORGIA ANNOTATED. THIS FORM DOES NOT IMPOSE A DUTY ON YOUR AGENT TO EXERCISE GRANTED POWERS; BUT, WHEN A POWER IS EXERCISED, YOUR AGENT WILL HAVE TO USE DUE CARE TO ACT FOR YOUR BENEFIT AND IN ACCORDANCE WITH THIS FORM. A COURT CAN TAKE AWAY THE POWERS OF YOUR AGENT IF IT FINDS THE AGENT IS NOT ACTING PROPERLY. YOU MAY NAME CO-AGENTS AND SUCCESSOR AGENTS UNDER THIS FORM, BUT YOU MAY NOT NAME A HEALTH CARE PROVIDER WHO MAY BE DIRECTLY OR INDIRECTLY INVOLVED IN RENDERING HEALTH CARE TO YOU UNDER THIS POWER. UNLESS YOU EXPRESSLY LIMIT THE DURATION OF THIS POWER IN THE MANNER PROVIDED BELOW OR UNTIL YOU REVOKE THIS POWER OR A COURT ACTING ON YOUR BEHALF TERMINATES IT, YOUR AGENT MAY EXERCISE THE POWERS GIVEN IN THIS POWER THROUGHOUT YOUR LIFETIME, EVEN AFTER YOU BECOME DISABLED, INCAPACITATED, OR INCOMPETENT. THE POWERS YOU GIVE YOUR AGENT, YOUR RIGHT TO REVOKE THOSE POWERS, AND THE PENALTIES FOR VIOLATING THE

* *www.caringinfo.com*

LAW ARE EXPLAINED MORE FULLY IN CODE SECTIONS 31-36-6, 31-36-9, AND 31-36-10 OF THE GEORGIA "DURABLE POWER OF ATTORNEY FOR HEALTH CARE ACT" OF WHICH THIS FORM IS A PART. THAT ACT EXPRESSLY PERMITS THE USE OF ANY DIFFERENT FORM OF POWER OF ATTORNEY YOU MAY DESIRE. IF THERE IS ANYTHING ABOUT THIS FORM THAT YOU DO NOT UNDERSTAND. YOU SHOULD ASK A LAWYER TO EXPLAIN IT TO YOU.

DURABLE POWER OF ATTORNEY made this day of, 20

1. I,   (name)

(address)

hereby appoint: (name of agent)

(address)

as my attorney in fact (my agent) to act for me and in my name in any way I could act in person to make any and all decisions for me concerning my personal care, medical treatment, hospitalization, and health care and to require, withhold, or withdraw any type of medical treatment or procedure, even though my death may ensue. My agent shall have the same access to my medical records that I have, including the right to disclose the contents to others. My agent shall also have full power to make a disposition of any part or all of my body for medical purposes, authorize an autopsy of my body, and direct the disposition of my remains.

(A reminder from National Hospice and Palliative Care Organization): THE ABOVE GRANT OF POWER IS INTENDED TO BE AS BROAD AS POSSIBLE SO THAT YOUR AGENT WILL HAVE AUTHORITY TO MAKE ANY DECISION YOU COULD MAKE TO OBTAIN OR TERMINATE ANY TYPE OF HEALTH CARE, INCLUDING WITHDRAWAL OF NOURISHMENT AND FLUIDS AND OTHER LIFE-SUSTAINING OR DEATH-DELAYING MEASURES, IF YOUR

AGENT BELIEVES SUCH ACTION WOULD BE CONSISTENT WITH YOUR INTENT AND DESIRES. IF YOU WISH TO LIMIT THE SCOPE OF YOUR AGENT'S POWERS OR PRESCRIBE SPECIAL RULES TO LIMIT THE POWER TO MAKE AN ANATOMICAL GIFT, AUTHORIZE AUTOPSY, OR DISPOSE OF REMAINS, YOU MAY DO SO IN THE FOLLOWING PARAGRAPHS.

2. The powers granted above shall not include the following powers or shall be subject to the following rules or limitations (here you may include any specific limitations you deem appropriate, such as your own definition of when life-sustaining or death-delaying measures should be withheld; a direction to continue nourishment and fluids or other life-sustaining or death-delaying treatment in all events; or instructions to refuse any specific types of treatment that are inconsistent with your religious beliefs or unacceptable to you for any other reason, such as blood transfusion, electroconvulsive therapy, or amputation):

(A reminder from National Hospice and Palliative Care Organization): THE SUBJECT OF LIFE-SUSTAINING OR DEATH-DELAYING TREATMENT IS OF PARTICULAR IMPORTANCE. FOR YOUR CONVENIENCE IN DEALING WITH THAT SUBJECT, SOME GENERAL STATEMENTS CONCERNING THE WITHHOLDING OR REMOVAL OF LIFE-SUSTAINING OR DEATH-DELAYING TREATMENT ARE SET FORTH BELOW. IF YOU AGREE WITH ONE OF THESE STATEMENTS, YOU MAY INITIAL THAT STATEMENT, BUT DO NOT INITIAL MORE THAN ONE:

I do not want my life to be prolonged, nor do I want life-sustaining or death-delaying treatment to be provided or continued if my agent believes the burdens of the treatment outweigh the expected benefits. I want my agent to consider the relief of suffering, the expense involved, and the quality as well as the possible extension of my life in making decisions concerning life-sustaining or death-delaying treatment.

I want my life to be prolonged and I want life-sustaining or death-delaying treatment to be provided or continued unless I am in a coma, including persistent vegetative state, which my attending physician believes to be irreversible, in accordance with reasonable medical standards at the time of reference. If and when I have suffered such an irreversible coma, I want life-sustaining or death-delaying treatment to be withheld or discontinued.

I want my life to be prolonged to the greatest extent possible without regard to my condition, the chances I have for recovery, or the cost of the procedures.

(A reminder from National Hospice and Palliative Care Organization): THIS POWER OF ATTORNEY MAY BE AMENDED OR REVOKED BY YOU AT ANY TIME AND IN ANY MANNER WHILE YOU ARE ABLE TO DO SO. IN THE ABSENCE OF AN AMENDMENT OR REVOCATION, THE AUTHORITY GRANTED IN THIS POWER OF ATTORNEY WILL BECOME EFFECTIVE AT THE TIME THIS POWER IS SIGNED AND WILL CONTINUE UNTIL YOUR DEATH AND WILL CONTINUE BEYOND YOUR DEATH IF ANATOMICAL GIFT, AUTOPSY, OR DISPOSITION OF REMAINS IS AUTHORIZED, UNLESS A LIMITATION ON THE BEGINNING DATE OR DURATION IS MADE BY INITIALING AND COMPLETING EITHER OR BOTH OF THE FOLLOWING:

3. ( ) This power of attorney shall become effective on (Insert a future date or event during your lifetime, such as court determination of your disability, incapacity, or incompetency, when you want this power to first take effect.)

4. ( ) This power of attorney shall terminate on (insert a future date or event, such as court determination of your disability, incapacity, or i ncompetency, when you want this power to terminate prior to your death.)

(A reminder from National Hospice and Palliative Care Organization): IF YOU WISH TO NAME SUCCESSOR AGENTS, INSERT THE NAMES AND ADDRESSES OF SUCH SUCCESSORS IN THE FOLLOWING PARAGRAPH:

5. If any agent named by me shall die, become legally disabled, incapacitated, or incompetent, or resign, refuse to act, or be unavailable, I name the following (each to act successively in the order named) as successors to such agent:

   1. Name

     Address

   2. Name

     Address

(A reminder from National Hospice and Palliative Care Organization): IF YOU WISH TO NAME A GUARDIAN OF YOUR PERSON IN THE EVENT A COURT DECIDES THAT ONE SHOULD BE APPOINTED, YOU MAY, BUT ARE NOT REQUIRED TO, DO SO BY INSERTING THE NAME OF SUCH GUARDIAN IN THE FOLLOWING PARAGRAPH. THE COURT WILL APPOINT THE PERSON NOMINATED BY YOU IF THE COURT FINDS THAT SUCH APPOINTMENT WILL SERVE YOUR BEST INTERESTS AND WELFARE. YOU MAY, BUT ARE NOT REQUIRED TO, NOMINATE AS YOUR GUARDIAN THE SAME PERSON NAMED IN THIS FORM AS YOUR AGENT.

6. If a guardian of my person is to be appointed, I nominate the following to serve as such guardian:

(name of guardian)

(address)

7. I am fully informed as to all the contents of this form and understand the full import of this grant of powers to my agent.

Signed:

(principal)

The principal has had an opportunity to read the above form and has signed the above form in our presence. We, the undersigned, each being over 18 years of age, witness the principal's signature at the request and in the presence of the principal, and in the presence of each other, on the day and year above set out.

Witness:

Address:

Witness:

Address:

Additional witness required when health care agency is signed in a hospital or skilled nursing facility. I hereby witness this health care agency and attest that I believe the principal to be of sound mind and to have made this health care agency willingly and voluntarily.

Witness (Attending Physician)

(signature)

Address

(A reminder from National Hospice and Palliative Care Organization): YOU MAY, BUT ARE NOT REQUIRED TO, REQUEST YOUR AGENT AND SUCCESSOR AGENTS TO PROVIDE SPECIMEN SIGNATURES BELOW. IF YOU INCLUDE SPECIMEN SIGNATURES IN THIS POWER

OF ATTORNEY, YOU MUST COMPLETE THE CERTIFICATION OPPOSITE THE SIGNATURES OF THE AGENTS.

Specimen signatures of agent and successor(s)

I certify that the signature of my agent and successor(s) is correct.

(agent)

(principal)

(successor agent)

(principal)

(successor agent)

(principal)

Courtesy of Caring Connections
1700 Diagonal Road, Suite 625, Alexandria, VA 22314
www.caringinfo.org. 800/658-8898

2005 National Hospice and Palliative Care Organization

Exhibit 6: Advance Directive*

Caring Connections, a program of the National Hospice and Palliative Care Organization, (NHPCO), is a national consumer engagement initiative to improve care at the end of life, supported by a grant from the Robert Wood Johnson Foundation.

The goal of Caring Connections is for consumers to hear a unified message promoting awareness and action for improved end-of-life care. Through these efforts, NHPCO seeks to support those working across the country to improve end-of-life care and conditions for all Americans.

Services from Caring Connections

Information and Advice Services

You can call our toll-free Helpline, 800/658–8898, if you need help completing your living will or health-care power of attorney, if you wish to talk to someone about how to plan for decisions you might face near the end of your life, or if you are dealing with a difficult end-of-life situation and need immediate information and advice. Below is just a sampling of the kinds of questions that we respond to:

- How do I complete my advance directives?
- What questions should I ask my mother's doctors about her care?
- My father's health-care providers will not honor his wishes. What shall I do?
- Do I have to be in pain?

Education Services

For the Public: We can provide publications and videos that offer practical information to educate consumers about how to get the best possible care

* *www.caringinfo.com*

near the end of life. We are building grassroots activities to help the public be involved in improving care for dying people. We also give consumers the opportunity to add their voices to the call for good end-of-life care.

For the Professionals: We can provide education and consultation to doctors, nurses, social workers, attorneys, clergy, and others. By becoming Partners, professional organizations gain access to a wide variety of materials and services that can help them improve end-of-life care in their institution or community.

Legal Services: Caring Connections tracks and monitors all state and federal legislation and significant court cases related to end-of-life care to ensure that our advance directives are always up to date, and to ensure that we are the source for the most up-to-date information about legislation and case law affecting end-of-life decision making and care.

Courtesy of Planning for Important Healthcare Decisions
Caring Connections,
1700 Diagonal Road, Suite 625, Alexandria, VA 22314
www.caringinfo.org. 800/658-8898

@ 2005 National Hospice and Palliative Care Organization

How to Use these Materials

1. Check to be sure that you have the materials for your state. You should complete a form for the state in which you expect to receive health care.
2. These materials include:
   - Instructions for preparing your advance directive
   - Your state-specific advance directive forms, which are the pages with the gray instruction bar on the left side
3. Read the instructions in their entirety. They give you specific information about the requirements in your state.
4. You may want to photocopy these forms before you start, so you will have a clean copy if you need to start over.
5. When you begin to complete the form, refer to the gray instruction bars—they indicate where you need to mark, insert your personal instructions, or sign the form.
6. Talk with your family, friends, and physicians about your decision to complete an advance directive. Be sure the person you appoint to make decision on your behalf understands your wishes.

If you have questions or need guidance in preparing your advance directive or about what you should do with it after you have completed it, you may call our toll free number 800/658-8898 and a staff member will be glad to assist you. For more information, contact: the National Hospice and Palliative Care Organization, 1700 Diagonal Road, Suite 625 Alexandria, VA 22314

Call our Helpline: 800/658-8898. Visit our website: www.caringinfo. org. Formerly a publication of Last Acts Partnership. Support for this program is provided by a grant from the Robert Wood Johnson Foundation, Princeton, New Jersey.

Exhibit 7: Introduction to Your Georgia Advance Directive*

This packet contains two legal documents that protect your right to refuse medical treatment you do not want, or to request treatment you do want, in the event you lose the ability to make decisions yourself:

1. The Georgia Durable Power of Attorney for Health Care lets you name someone to make decisions about your medical care—including decisions about life support—if you can no longer speak for yourself. The Durable Power of Attorney for Health Care is especially useful because it appoints someone to speak for you any time you are unable to make your own medical decisions, not only at the end of life.
2. The Georgia Living Will lets you state your wishes about medical care in the event that you are terminally ill, in a persistent vegetative state, or coma and can no longer make your own medical decisions. Your diagnosis must be certified in writing by your doctor and one other physician.

Caring Connections recommends that you complete both of these documents to best ensure that you receive the medical care you want when you can no longer speak for yourself.

Note: These documents will be legally binding only if the person completing them is a competent adult (at least 18 years old).

@ 2005 National Hospice and Palliative Care Organization

* *www.caringinfo.com*

Exhibit 8: Georgia Durable Power of Attorney for Health Care*

Whom should I appoint as my agent? Your agent is the person you appoint to make decisions about your medical care if you become unable to make those decisions yourself. Your agent can be a family member or a close friend whom you trust to make serious decisions. The person you name as your agent should clearly understand your wishes and be willing to accept the responsibility of making medical decisions for you. An agent may also be called an "attorney-in-fact" or "proxy." No health-care provider may act as your agent if they are directly or indirectly involved in your health care.

You can appoint a second and third person as your alternate agent(s). The alternate will step in if the first person you name as agent is unable, unwilling, or unavailable to act for you.

How do I make my Georgia Durable Power of Attorney for Health Care legal?

The law requires that you sign your document, or direct another to sign it, in the presence of two witnesses who must be at least eighteen years of age. If you are a patient in a hospital or skilled nursing facility, your document must also be signed in the presence of your doctor.

Note: You do not need to notarize your Georgia Durable Power of Attorney for Health Care.

Should I add personal instructions to my Georgia Durable Power of Attorney for Health Care?

Caring Connections advises you not to add instructions to this document. One of the strongest reasons for naming an agent is to have someone who can respond flexibly as your medical situation changes and deal with situations that you did not foresee. If you add instructions to this document, you might unintentionally restrict your agent's power

* *www.caringinfo.com*

to act in your best interest. Instead we urge you to talk with your agent about your future medical care and describe what you consider to be an acceptable "quality of life." If you want to record your wishes about specific treatments or conditions, you should use your Georgia Living Will.

What if I change my mind?

You may revoke your Georgia Durable Power of Attorney for Health Care at any time, regardless of your mental or physical condition, by:

- obliterating, burning, tearing, or otherwise destroying or defacing your document,
- signing and dating a written revocation or directing another person to do so, or
- orally revoking your document in the presence of a witness, at least eighteen years of age, who must sign and date a written confirmation of your revocation within thirty days.

If you get married after completing a Durable Power of Attorney for Health Care in which you have not named your spouse as your agent, your marriage automatically revokes the power of your agent. If you have appointed your spouse as your agent and your marriage ends, your agent's power is automatically revoked.

What other important facts should I know?

Section 6 of your Durable Power of Attorney for Health Care provides space where you can nominate someone to serve as your guardian if there should come a time when you need a court-appointed guardian. Unless a court specifies otherwise, your guardian has no power to make any personal or health care decisions granted to your agent under your Durable Power of Attorney for Health Care.

@ 2005 National Hospice and Palliative Care Organization

Exhibit 9: Completing Your Georgia Living Will*

How do I make my living will legal?

The law requires that you sign your living will in the presence of two witnesses, who must also sign the document to show that they personally know you and believe you to be of sound mind, that you signed the document in their presence, that they are eighteen years of age or older, and that they do not fall into any of the categories of people who cannot be witnesses.

These witnesses cannot:

- be related to you by blood or marriage,
- be financially responsible for your medical care,
- be entitled to any part of your estate upon your death,
- have a claim against any portion of your estate,
- be your doctor or a person employed by your doctor, or
- be an employee of a health-care facility in which you are a patient.

If you are a patient in a hospital or skilled nursing facility, you are required to have a third witness. If you are in a hospital, this third witness must be either the chief of the medical staff, a staff physician, or another person designated by the hospital administrator. If you are in a skilled nursing facility, this third witness must be either the medical director or a physician on the medical staff. Your third witness cannot be involved in your medical care.

Note: You do not need to notarize your Georgia Living Will.

Can I add personal instructions to my living will?

Yes. You can add personal instructions in the part of the document called "other directions." For example, you may want to refuse specific treatments by a statement such as, "I especially do not want cardiopulmonary resuscitation, a respirator, or antibiotics." You may also want to emphasize

* *www.caringinfo.com*

pain control by adding instructions such as, "I want to receive as much pain medication as necessary to ensure my comfort, even if it may hasten my death." If you want to refuse artificial nutrition, artificial hydration, or both, you must check the appropriate options in section 1. If you have appointed an agent and you want to add personal instructions to your living will, it is a good idea to write a statement such as, "Any questions about how to interpret or when to apply my living will are to be decided by my agent."

It is important to learn about the kinds of life-sustaining treatment you might receive. Consult your doctor or order the Caring Connections booklet *Advance Directives and End-of-Life Decisions.*

What if I change my mind?

You can revoke your Georgia Living Will at any time, regardless of your mental condition, by:

–   destroying the document,
–   signing and dating a written revocation, or directing another person to do so in your presence, or
–   orally or otherwise expressing your intent to revoke your living will.

Your doctor must be notified of your revocation for it to be effective.

What other important facts should I know?

If you are a woman of childbearing age and would like your Georgia Living Will to be honored even if you are pregnant, you must initial the statement in paragraph 5 of the living will form.

State law requires that before honoring a pregnant patient's living will, the attending physician must first determine whether the fetus is viable. If the fetus is viable, your living will would not be honored, even if you initial paragraph 5. If this issue concerns you, contact Caring Connections for more information.

@ 2005 National Hospice and Palliative Care Organization

Exhibit 10: After You Have Completed Your Documents*

1. Your Georgia Durable Power of Attorney for Health Care and Georgia Living Will are important legal documents. Keep the original signed documents in a secure but accessible place. Do not put the original documents in a safe deposit box or any other security box that would keep others from having access to them.

2. Give photocopies of the signed originals to your agent and alternate agents, doctor(s), family, close friends, clergy, and anyone else who might become involved in your health care. If you enter a nursing home or hospital, have photocopies of your documents placed in your medical records.

3. Be sure to talk to your agent and alternates, doctor(s), clergy, and family and friends about your wishes concerning medical treatment. Discuss your wishes with them often, particularly if your medical condition changes.

4. If you want to make changes to your documents after they have been signed and witnessed, you must complete new documents.

5. Remember, you can always revoke one or both of your Georgia documents.

6. Be aware that your Georgia documents will not be effective in the event of a medical emergency. Ambulance personnel are required to provide cardiopulmonary resuscitation (CPR) unless they are given a separate order that states otherwise. These orders, commonly called "non-hospital do-not-resuscitate orders," are designed for people whose poor health gives them little chance of benefiting from CPR. These orders must be signed by your physician and instruct ambulance personnel not to attempt CPR if your heart or breathing should stop. Currently not all states have laws authorizing non-hospital do-not-resuscitate orders.

* *www.caringinfo.com*

Caring Connections does not distribute these forms. We suggest you speak to your physician.

If you would like more information about this topic, contact Caring Connections or consult the Caring Connections booklet *Cardiopulmonary Resuscitation, Do-Not Resuscitate Orders and End-Of-Life Decisions.*

@ 2005 National Hospice and Palliative Care Organization

Appendix C

Exhibit 1: General Information

*The following are samples of some of the pages of the information that would be included in the book *Putting Your House in Order: A Vital Tool for Properly Managing Your Estate* when completing the forms.

Name:

Social Security Number:

Date of Birth: /   /

Birthplace:

Home Address:

City:

State: Zip Code: County:

Spouse's Name:

Social Security Number:

Date of Birth: /   /

Birthplace:

Marriage

Date:

City:

State: Zip Code: Country:

Exhibit 2: Quick Reference List

This information is designed to assist a spouse, a caregiver, or an executor during an extended illness, injury, or death. This section should allow an individual to step in and start locating names, numbers, and addresses immediately without wasting time and energy.

Name of Home Alarm Company:
Password Code:
Account Number:
Telephone Number:
Location of Mailbox:
Mailbox Number:
Key Location or Combination Number:
Residence Keys:
Who Has Keys—Name of Individual:
Telephone Number:
Residence Keys:
Who Has Keys—Name of Individual:
Telephone Number:
Name of Pet Sitter:
Pet's Name:
Telephone Number:
Address:
City:
State: Zip Code:

Name of Dog Walker:
Pet's Name:
Telephone Number:
Address:
City:
State: Zip Code:

Name of Pet Medications:
Pet's Name:
Location of Prescription:

Name of Veterinarian:
Telephone Number:
Address:
City:
State: Zip Code:

Name of Electric Company:
Account Number:
Telephone Number:
Name of Gas/Propane Company:
Account Number:
Telephone Number:

Name of Garbage Collection Company:
Pickup Day:
Account Number:
Telephone Number:

Name of Recycling Company:
Pickup Day:
Account Number:
Telephone Number:

Name of Cable/Satellite Television Company:
Account Number:
Telephone Number:

Name of Telephone Company:
Account Number:
Telephone Number:

Name of Cellular Telephone Company:
Account Number:
Telephone Number:

Name of Internet Provider:
Account Number:
Telephone Number:

Name of Pest/Termite Control Company:
Account Number:
Telephone Number:

Name of Storage Building Company:
Storage Compartment Number:
Telephone Number:
Rental Agreement Type: Month to Month/Yearly
Property Address:
City:
State: Zip Code:

Exhibit 3: Documents at a Glance

This organizer is a great time-saver. By listing if the document is an original or copy and by including the location, one can save hours of looking for a document that might not even be available.

Document Legend: Original = O | Copy = C | Unavailable = U | Location = where the item is located

Personal Information for:
Marriage Certificate O C U Location:
Birth Certificate(s) O C U Location:
Social Security Card(s) O C U Location:
Health Insurance Card O C U Location:
Life Insurance Policy(s) O C U Location:
Will O C U Location:
Power of Attorney O C U Location:
Advance Directives O C U Location:
Discharge from Military DD214 O C U Location:
Military Records O C U Location:
Naturalization (Citizenship) Papers O C U Location:
Organization Memberships O C U Location:

Exhibit 4: Funeral

Below are two of the questions to assist those involved in making your final arrangements.

Are funeral services prepaid? List of prepaid services and location of receipt for verification:

Are you a military veteran? Military veterans are entitled to free burial in a national cemetery and to a grave marker. For additional information, visit the Department of Veterans Affairs' website, www.cem.va.gov. To reach the regional veterans office in your area, call 1-800-827-1000.

Funeral Home:
Address:
City:
State: Zip Code:
Telephone Number:

Life/Pension/Retirement Insurance
Name of Insurance Company:
Insured:
Policy/Account Number:
Amount:
Beneficiary:
Telephone Number:

Life/Pension/Retirement Insurance
Name of Insurance Company:
Insured:
Policy/Account Number:
Amount:
Beneficiary:
Telephone Number:

Life/Pension/Retirement Insurance
Name of Insurance Company:
Insured:
Policy/Account Number:
Amount:
Beneficiary:
Telephone Number:

Burial Insurance
Name of Insurance Company:
Insured:
Policy/Account Number:
Amount:
Beneficiary:
Telephone Number:

Cemetery Plot
Plot Number:
I would like to be buried next to:
Address:
City:
State: Zip Code:

Casket
Type of Material: Wood or Metal
Outside Color:

Headstone
I would like my headstone to say:
I would like a picture of _____ on my headstone.

Cremation Services
Are services prepaid?
List of prepaid services and location of receipt for verification:

Address:

City:

State: Zip Code:

Telephone Number:

Urn

Type of Container:

Wording on Container:

Container is to be placed:

I would like my services to be officiated by:

Name and Title:

Telephone Number:

Address:

City:

State: Zip Code:

I would like my services to be conducted at:

Name of Facility:

Telephone Number:

Address:

City:

Exhibit 5: Assets

Assets are usually defined as everything that you own. An asset is a possession that can be given an assessed financial value. Assets come in all kinds of shapes and sizes. If you have particular items that you would like to be given to an individual(s), discuss this with your attorney. Because of varying state laws, they can guide you so that your wish might be fulfilled.

Personal Information for:
Last Updated:

Life Insurance
Name of Insurance Company:
Insured:
Policy/Account Number:
Amount:
Beneficiary:
Telephone Number:
Joint Ownership (if yes, list who):
Name of Insurance Company:
Insured:
Policy/Account Number:
Amount:
Beneficiary:
Telephone Number:
Joint Ownership (if yes, list who):
Name of Insurance Company:
Insured:
Policy/Account Number:
Amount:
Beneficiary:
Telephone Number:
Joint Ownership (if yes, list who):

Pension Death Benefits
Name of Insurance Company:
Insured:
Policy/Account Number:
Amount:
Beneficiary:
Telephone Number:
Joint Ownership (if yes, list who):

Bank Accounts
(savings, checking, safe deposit box)
Name of Bank:
Account Number:
Type of Account:
Address:
City:
State: Zip Code:
Joint Ownership (if yes, list who):
Name of Bank:
Account Number:
Type of Account:
Address:
City:
State: Zip Code:

Exhibit 6: Liabilities

Liabilities are usually defined as everything that one owes or is still making payments on. Credit is borrowed money that one uses to purchase items and then repays within an agreed-upon time frame. The average American has four credit cards. One in seven Americans carries more than ten credit cards. None of us are like Walter Cavanagh. He at one time had 1,497 valid credit cards, which gave him access to more than $1.7 million in credit.

Personal Information for:

Last updated:

Bank Loans

Name of Institution:

Account Number:

Type of Account:

Telephone Number:

Address:

City:

State: Zip Code:

Joint Ownership (if yes, list who):

Name of Institution:

Account Number:

Type of Account:

Telephone Number:

Address:

City:

State: Zip Code:

Joint Ownership (if yes, list who):

Car Loans

Name of Institution:

Account Number:

Type of Account:

Telephone Number:

Exhibit 7: Family History

Carmine and Marietta came from a small city in southern Italy almost one hundred years ago. Their love was strong, and they wanted to be married and live in America. Time was on their side, but patience was not. They wanted to go to America quickly. Carmine had just turned nineteen years of age, and Marietta was only weeks shy of her eighteenth birthday. They had their whole lives in front of them, but they wanted to fulfill their dream then. It had taken them months and months of saving every penny they earned, and they still did not have enough for tickets to America. The ride across the open seas would take almost two weeks and was costly. They were able to borrow the remaining sum so they could purchase their dream: two tickets to the United States of America. The voyage was long and bumpy. They arrived on time ten days later. They were facing the Statue of Liberty as the ship pulled into the dock. They disembarked the ship and traveled through Ellis Island to begin their dream together. Do you like that story? If the information about Carmine and Marietta had not been written down by one of their daughters, it would have been lost forever. Create a family history. Pass along those bits of information and stories that you always meant to share with others.

Personal Information for:
Names of Parents:
Father:
Ethnic Background:
Birthplace:
City: State: Country:
Occupation:
Mother:
Ethnic Background:
Birthplace:
City: State: Country:
Occupation:

Names of Maternal Grandparents:
Grandfather:
Ethnic Background:
Birthplace:
City: State: Country:
Occupation:
Grandmother:
Ethnic Background:
Birthplace:
City: State: Country:
Occupation:
Names of Fraternal Grandparents:
Grandfather:
Grandmother:
Notes:

Appendix D

Home and Safety Modification Checklist[114]

Security

- ☐ Post important numbers in an easy-to-read format beside all telephones.
- ☐ Check to determine if all window and door locks are operable.
- ☐ If the family member wanders outside the home, install chain locks out of reach.
- ☐ Consider a commercially monitored emergency alert system if the elderly family member lives at home alone the majority of the time.
- ☐ Be sure to have extra keys and combinations of all locks for emergency purposes. If possible, give a set of keys to a nearby trusted friend who can also help out in an emergency.

Around the House

- ☐ Pick up all throw rugs, scatter rugs, or mats so they do not cause an accident by slipping on or tripping over them.
- ☐ Be sure that all fixtures have the proper-size light bulb and are in working condition.
- ☐ Check the furnace to be sure it is working properly and clean out the filters.
- ☐ Be sure to regularly check all fire alarms to be sure they are in working condition.
- ☐ Keep extra batteries for the most commonly used items.
- ☐ Lower the hot water to 120 degrees or lower to prevent burns.
- ☐ Rearrange furniture for larger areas and more space to move around.

---

[114] This list was designed by the author.

☐ If holding, turning, or grabbing doorknobs is difficult, change door handles to long-handled levers.

☐ Repair uneven and broken concrete steps, sidewalks, and other walking areas.

☐ Install railings by outdoor steps.

☐ Keep steps, sidewalks, and other walking areas free from leaves, snow, and ice.

☐ Lock basement doors.

☐ Consider an alarm to let you know when a door is opened.

Bathroom

☐ Place nonskid strips in all tubs and showers.

☐ Place a nonskid bath mat next to shower and tub.

☐ Install grab bars around in the bathtub/shower and by the toilet to assist in standing.

☐ Check all towel bars are secured tightly.

☐ Be sure there are no electrical appliances in the bathroom.

☐ A raised toilet seat may help if the individual has difficulties getting up.

☐ Be sure all faucets are well marked.

☐ If holding, turning, or grabbing items is difficult, change faucet handles to long-handled faucet levers.

Kitchen

☐ Remove stove and oven knobs if the elderly individual is confused or cognitively impaired. Store these items out of reach so they do not turn on these appliances and injure themselves.

☐ Put the most commonly used kitchen items in an easy-to-reach location. Having to reach up too high or bend too low to get kitchens items can also initiate an accident or injury.

☐ Keep electrical appliances away from the sink.

- ☐ Store sharp knives and utensils in a safe location.
- ☐ Remove step stools.
- ☐ Keep towels and flammable items away from the stove.
- ☐ Put a fire extinguisher in the kitchen.

Bedrooms

- ☐ Keep a flashlight, telephone, and lamp at the bedside for easy reach.
- ☐ Consider installing handrails in the hallway and between the bedroom and bathroom if ambulation is unsteady.

Stairs and Hallways

- ☐ If climbing stairs is too difficult, consider relocating the individuals' bedroom to the main floor. A stair glide is also an option that can assist the elderly going up and down the steps.
- ☐ Keep stairs and hallways free of clutter.
- ☐ Install handrails the complete length of the stairway.
- ☐ Install nonskid strips on uncarpeted areas.
- ☐ Remove all step and floor coverings that are ripped or in poor condition.